VENTING
MADE EASY

Rhyming Stuff for Progressives
And Other Thinking Individuals

VAL RICHARDSON

PAGE PUBLISHING, INC.
New York, NY

First originally published by Page Publishing, Inc. 2018

ISBN 978-1-64350-413-1 (Paperback)
ISBN 978-1-64350-414-8 (Digital)

Printed in the United States of America

CONTENTS

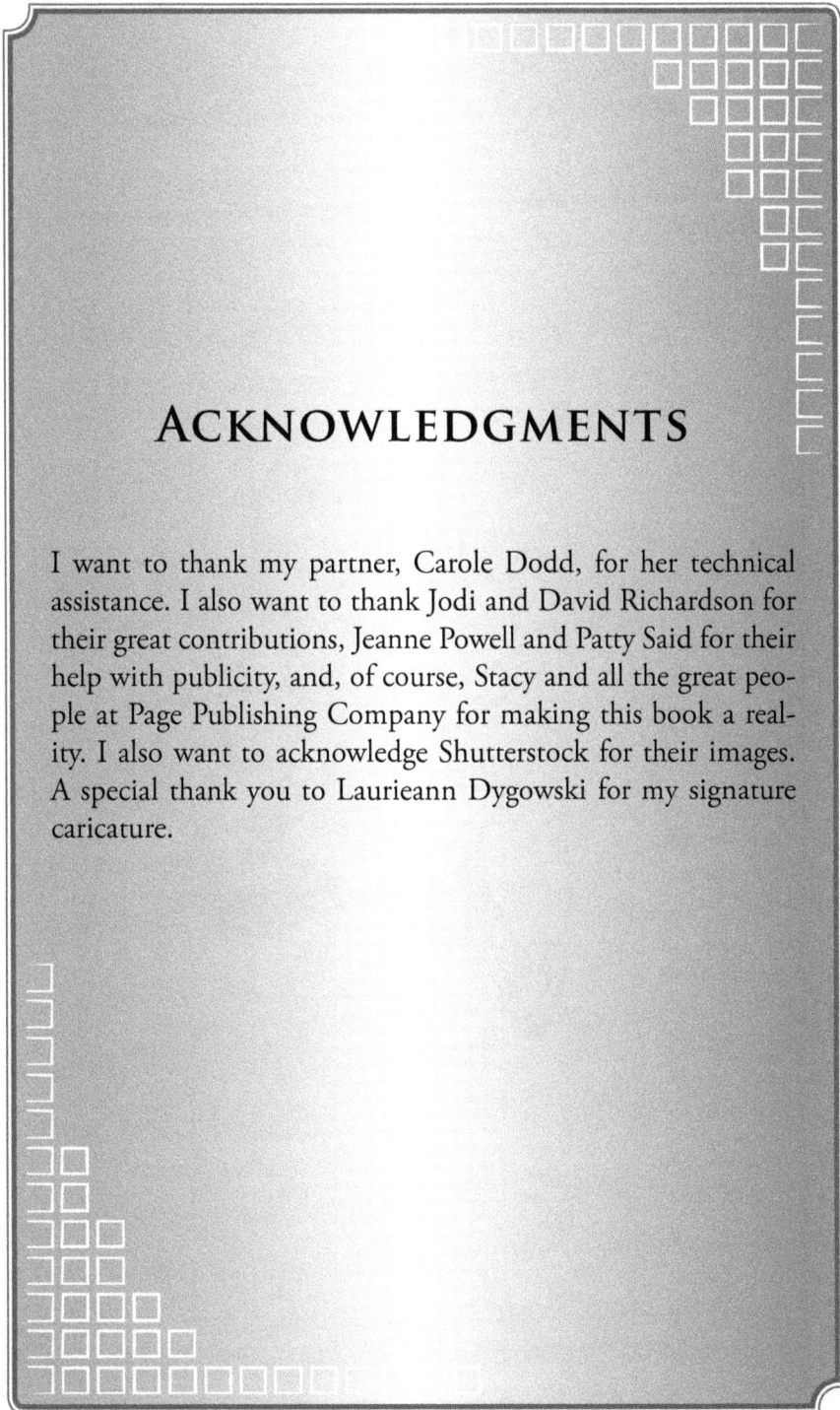

ACKNOWLEDGMENTS

I want to thank my partner, Carole Dodd, for her technical assistance. I also want to thank Jodi and David Richardson for their great contributions, Jeanne Powell and Patty Said for their help with publicity, and, of course, Stacy and all the great people at Page Publishing Company for making this book a reality. I also want to acknowledge Shutterstock for their images. A special thank you to Laurieann Dygowski for my signature caricature.

INTRODUCTION

Y'all sit down
So you can read
Every rhyme
Without a frown.

The pendulum swings
It causes anger
It causes hope.
When it swings away
It will swing back
If we get out the vote.

If you care about the country,
Not to vote would be a pity.
Even though I'm ninety-one
I always vote on day 1.

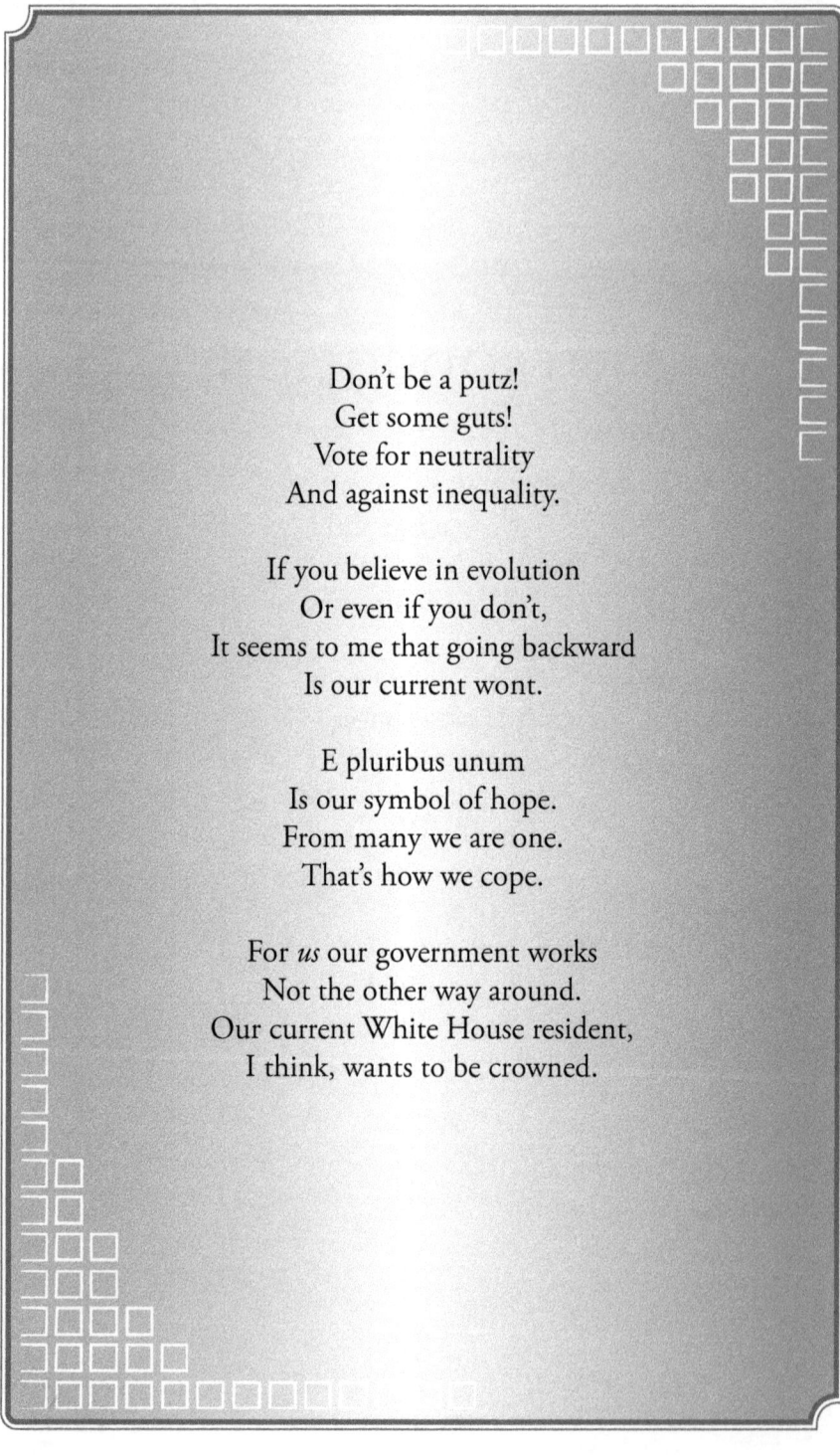

Don't be a putz!
Get some guts!
Vote for neutrality
And against inequality.

If you believe in evolution
Or even if you don't,
It seems to me that going backward
Is our current wont.

E pluribus unum
Is our symbol of hope.
From many we are one.
That's how we cope.

For *us* our government works
Not the other way around.
Our current White House resident,
I think, wants to be crowned.

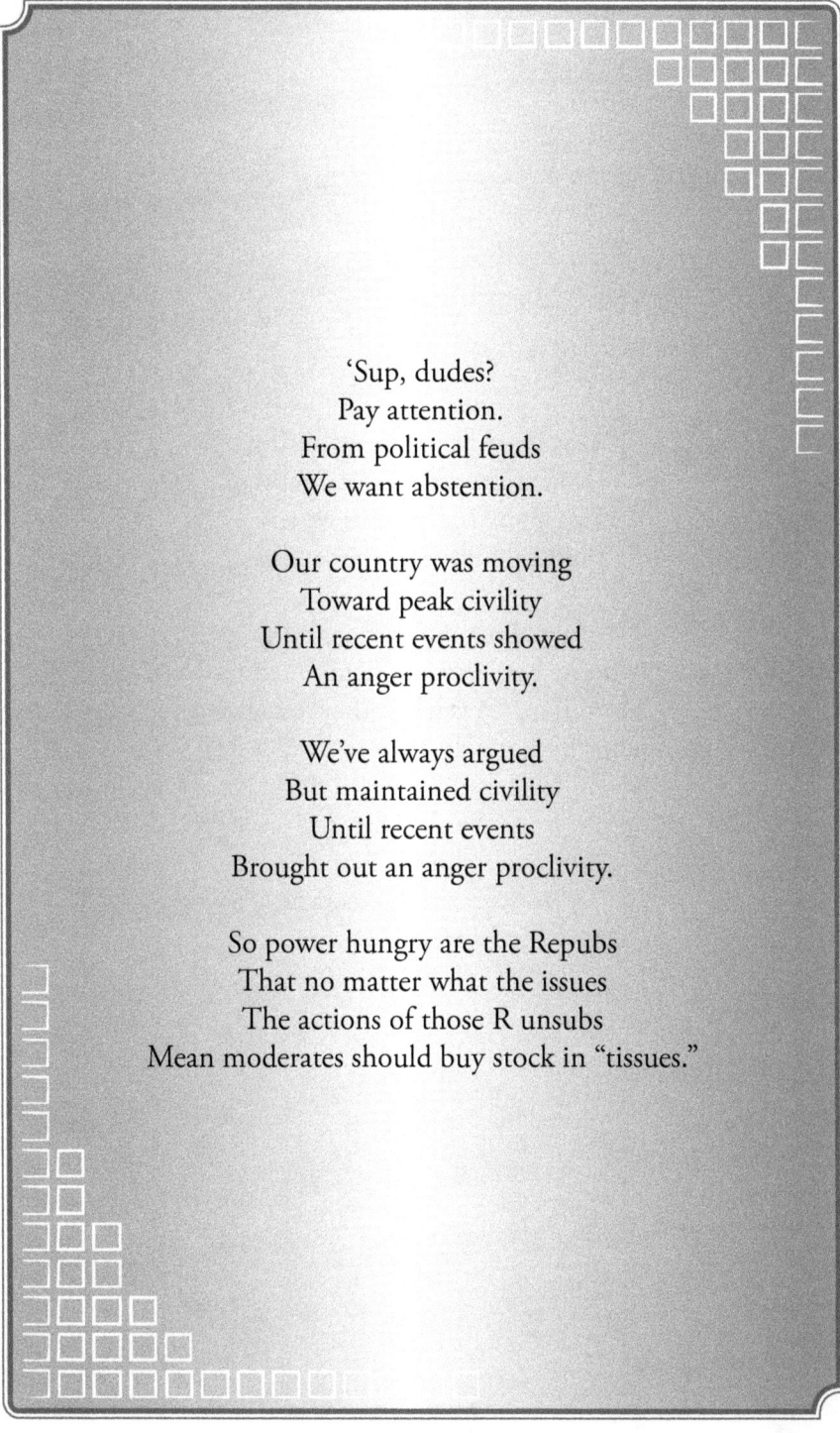

'Sup, dudes?
Pay attention.
From political feuds
We want abstention.

Our country was moving
Toward peak civility
Until recent events showed
An anger proclivity.

We've always argued
But maintained civility
Until recent events
Brought out an anger proclivity.

So power hungry are the Repubs
That no matter what the issues
The actions of those R unsubs
Mean moderates should buy stock in "tissues."

If you are prone to twittering,
Don't waste time just frittering.
Pass along the rhymes we send.
Political hubris has got to end.

Not all Democrats are pure.
Some have dirt on them for sure.
The difference is when they're exposed
They have the decency to be deposed.

By the hair
Of your chinny chin chin,
To save our democracy
Moderates must win.

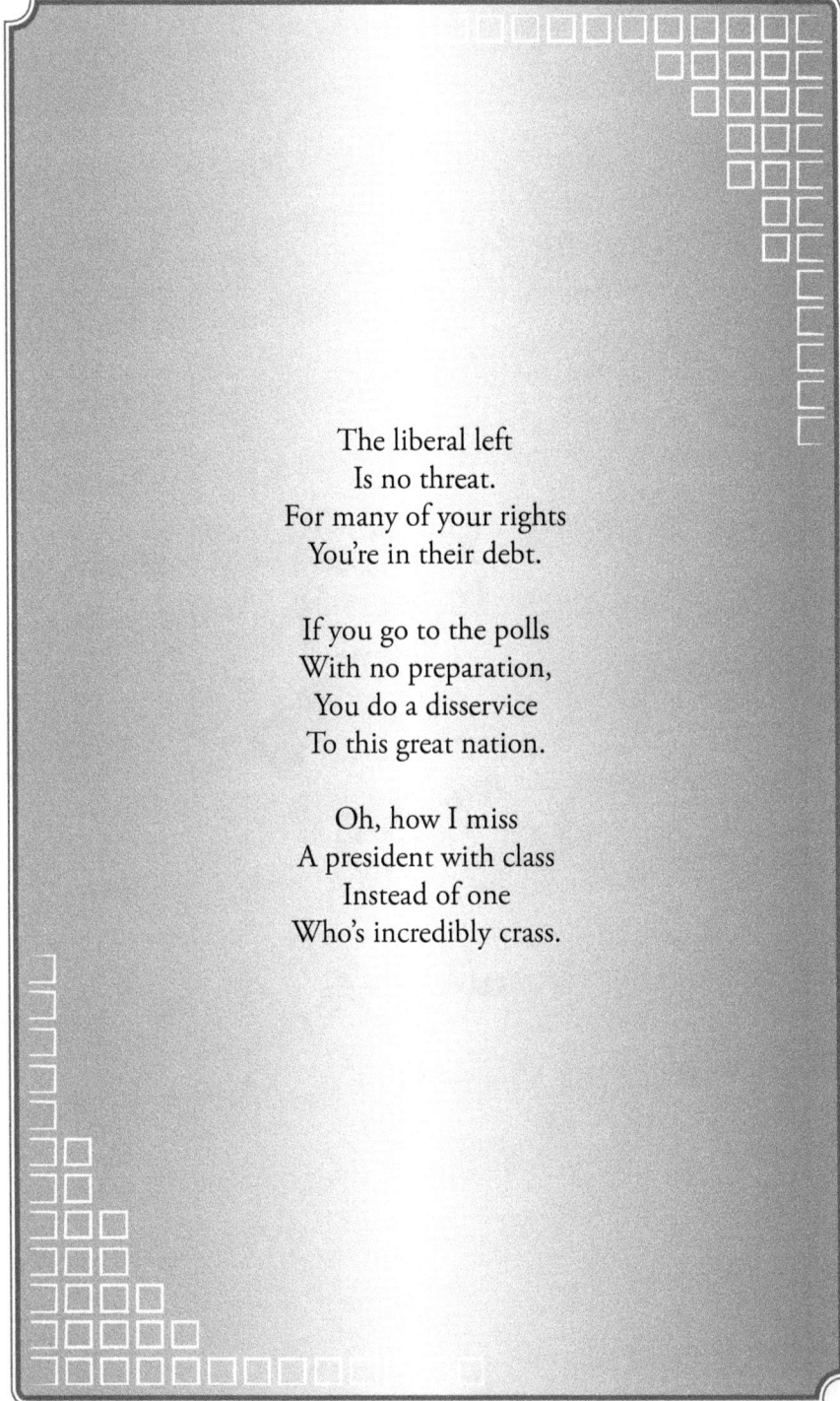

The liberal left
Is no threat.
For many of your rights
You're in their debt.

If you go to the polls
With no preparation,
You do a disservice
To this great nation.

Oh, how I miss
A president with class
Instead of one
Who's incredibly crass.

Where, oh where
Has my president gone?
Where, oh where
Can he be?
Obama's long gone
And oh, how I long
For him
To return to me!

The Trump administration
Is such a pain
From tearing our hair
We must refrain.

We look askance
At the Republican dance.
They wiggle and squirm
But still hold firm
Trying to save their ances.

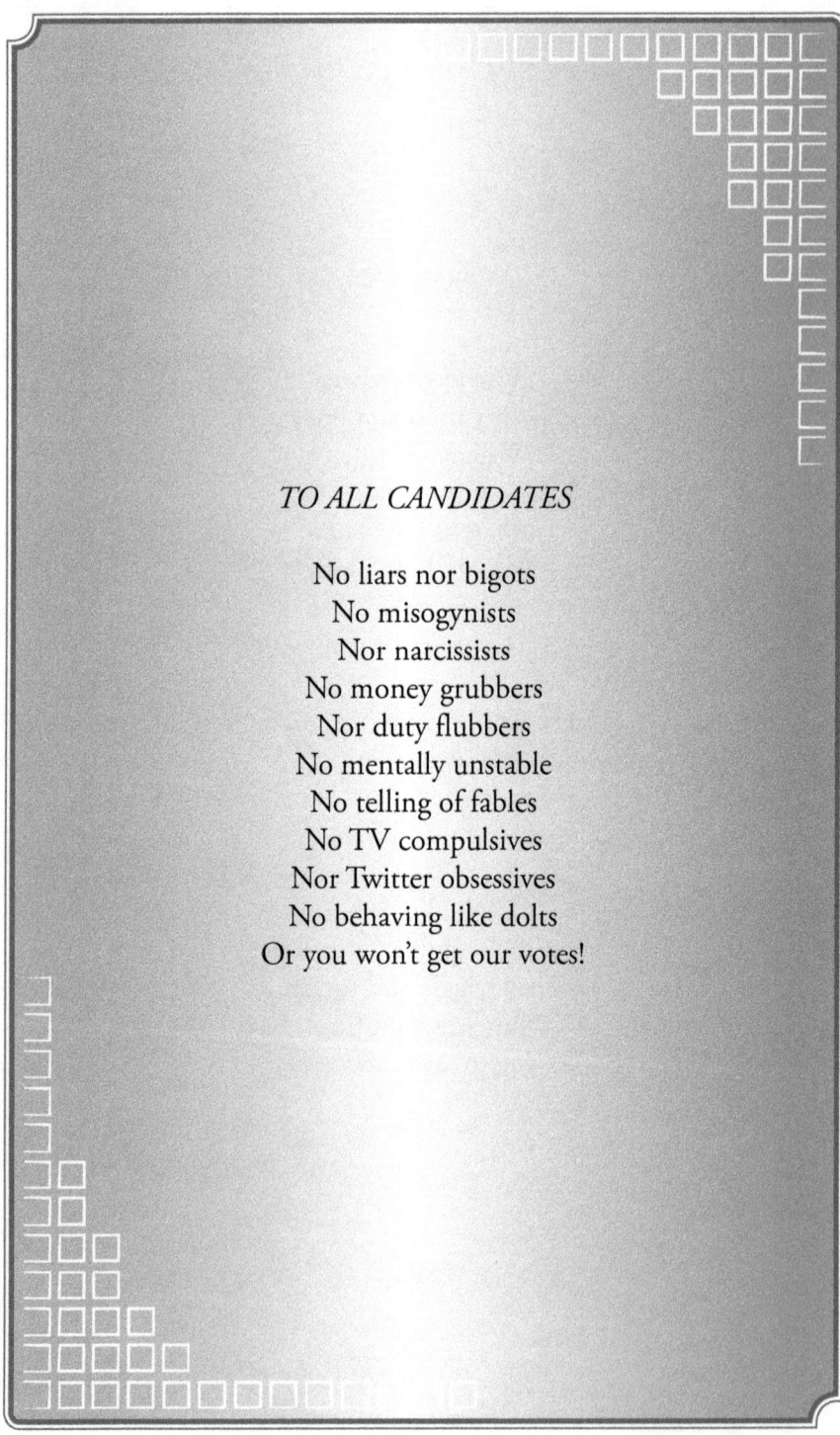

TO ALL CANDIDATES

No liars nor bigots
No misogynists
Nor narcissists
No money grubbers
Nor duty flubbers
No mentally unstable
No telling of fables
No TV compulsives
Nor Twitter obsessives
No behaving like dolts
Or you won't get our votes!

BIPARTISANSHIP

Even a smidge
Of bipartisanship
Would help bridge
The ideology chasm.

Work together! Work together!
It's so important you work together.
Your ego trips and power grabs
Feel to us like picking scabs.

Let's all work together
If you love democracy.
To do otherwise
Is obvious hypocrisy.

The left hand giveth
And the right taketh away,
But we could work together
In a more constructive way.

THE CABINET AND LEGISLATIVE BODY

Three branches of government
Each with a function.
The president is one and
Must act with compunction.

Take all the bottom-feeders
And let them work for me.
That fulfills my promise
To drain the swamp, you see.

Ethics in government
Should be a must.
Currently both houses
Fill us with disgust.

Government is only
As good as its reps.
Do your research
So you make no missteps.

Finally, our legislature
Has found some spine.
They voted to keep sanctions
And with that I'm just fine.

Until our legislators
Accept responsibility
We'll never have
Any tranquility.

Let's have one bill, one vote
With no extraneous additions.
It would save time, we should note,
And be a far less confusing rendition.

The Senate's addicted
To altercation,
But that only leads
To obfuscation.

This president's cabinet
All seem to think (so rank)
That taxpayers' funds are
Their personal piggy bank.

Poor helpless Pruitt.
Afraid of a little shouting.
He had to fly first-class
Because he couldn't help pouting.

Taxpayers were given the billing
For Pruitt to travel first-class
On planes with passengers crass
Who told him our planet he's killing.

"You play, you pay!"
Should be taxpayers' cry.
These sexual offenders
Should be hung out to dry.

Of Maxine Waters Trump opined
That she needed an IQ test.
I'm sure she wouldn't mind.
She could take the adult one,
Not the children's version
That Trump does best.

I'm a fan of Elizabeth Warren.
Not afraid to speak up.
When ordered to "sit down."
On the outside she did.
On the inside she didn't.

CHURCHES AND RELIGION

I admit I am confounded
Yes, actually dumbfounded,
Why those who believe in a gentle Jesus
Follow instead such a violent cuss.

The god of the alt-right
Is not found in the Bible,
And I am more than sad-sacked
By religion being hijacked.

Following the golden rule
Makes it easier to see
How we can make concessions
Without a referee.

Hate rhetoric
Helps separate.
More civil language
We must contemplate.

I'm mad at the pope.
He took me to task.
So I'll worship Putin.
With him I can cope.

The First Amendment rights.
The far right wants to negate
The First Amendment's
Separation of church and state.

Allowing churches to endorse
(Tax-free) their candidates,
Fills constitutionalists with remorse
About the merging of church and state.

Christians talk of "free will."
But will is only free
If there's a choice.

Voting for an abortion ban
Is really just a control scam.

Christian conservatives
Seem oddly to surmise
Returning to the Crusades
Would be a welcome surprise.

Drank the wine.
Ate the bread.
Went to confession.
All is forgiven.

Economy

If you think the economy is tumblin'
Even though Wall Street is bubblin',
Consider moving to Ireland
Where your "capital is always Dublin."

Money! Money! Money!
We need it for catastrophes,
But Congress says it's more expedient
To cut taxes on the 1 percent!

Big money can corrupt.
Public financing of
Campaigns would disrupt
Big money's control of elections.

Come to my cabinet.
Here's your desk
With its piggy bank drawer
Full of taxpayer funds
For you to explore
So go ahead
And travel some more.

Environment

Climate change defiers
Are science deniers.

When T removed Obama's ban
On toxic waste and stuff
To protect the land he had no plan
From the harm that's done by man.

Ashes to ashes,
Dust to dust.
Keep the US green
Or we'll all go bust.

Hurricane Harvey
Is absolute proof
That science saves lives.
Without it, we goof.

During his trip to oversee
The areas hit by Harvey
Trump said he agrees
That government must help.
But then the Republicans
Cut funding for catastrophes.

What has to happen
For the far right to perceive
Global warming is real
And to show they believe?

There's no need
For long reflection
To know we need
Consumer protection.

A ban keeping our rivers and lakes
Free from toxic waste
Was rescinded by Trump.
Now it's OK to dump.

Bad decisions Trump is amassing.
His ignorance is all-encompassing.
He runs roughshod
Both here and abroad
Over everything good that's been passing.

Trump lifted the ban
On toxic waste
And that ignorant plan
Threatens animals and man.

Of things scientific Trump has no clue.
Out of his mouth untruths he doth spew.
The election hit us out of the blue.
Now we are in a primordial stew.

China, which used to be backward
And has the air to prove it,
Now's switching from coal to solar.
We could do it if we had their grit.

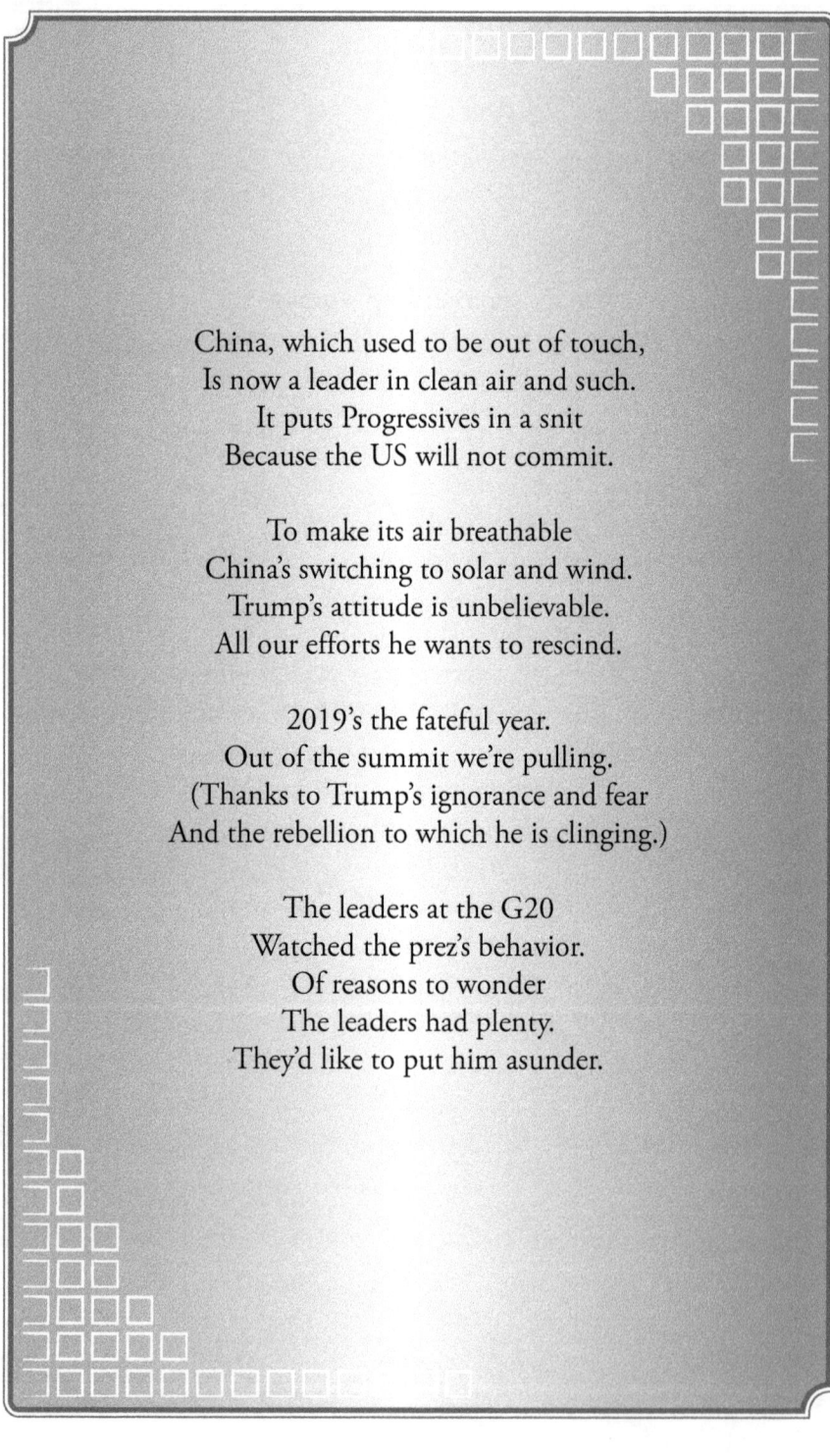

China, which used to be out of touch,
Is now a leader in clean air and such.
It puts Progressives in a snit
Because the US will not commit.

To make its air breathable
China's switching to solar and wind.
Trump's attitude is unbelievable.
All our efforts he wants to rescind.

2019's the fateful year.
Out of the summit we're pulling.
(Thanks to Trump's ignorance and fear
And the rebellion to which he is clinging.)

The leaders at the G20
Watched the prez's behavior.
Of reasons to wonder
The leaders had plenty.
They'd like to put him asunder.

Our rivers and lakes
Depend on you.
Elect science believers
Who will do what it takes.

The way to go
Is from coal to wind
And from wind to solar.
But Trump's too thin-skinned.
Gives me pains in my plexus solar.

Trump's obsession with coal
Is already taking its toll.
No miners have been trained
Or sustainable jobs gained.
It's very bad policy on the whole.

When Trump badmouths the EPA
We need our castor oil.
We should be switching to wind and solar
But to dirty coal he is loyal.

Trump is taking us backward
At a furious pace.
His behavior's a danger
To the whole human race.

Toxic waste in the water
(The lakes and the streams).
Removing Barack's order
Is killing our dreams.

Reforesting the earth
Is of inestimable worth:
For air oxygenating
We're now supplicating.
Seed bombing could mean rebirth.

Someday Trump may get
The credit he so craves
When our planet
Can no longer be saved.
Then he might wish
The credit to waive.

GERRYMANDERING

Burkett is for gerrymandering
Because it favors her party.
As head of the committee
She refused to allow a vote.

Burkett, in charge of redistricting,
Thinks it's OK to win elections
By partisan rigging.

On gerrymandering Burkett wouldn't act.
To stay in power, she made a pact.
She kept the bill in her committee.
And that really is the nitty-gritty.

On fair redistricting
Burkett refused to act.
Now a federal judge
Says Texas must. It's fact.

Gerrymander! Gerrymander!
That's their game
For winning elections.
They all bear much blame.

Gerrymandering's zigging
And zagging of districts
To favor one party
Is election rigging.

GUNS AND VIOLENCE

More than prayers,
We need action;
No assault weapons,
No high count clips,
Do background checks,
And hobble the NRA.

No child should have to run
From a dangerous gun,
But Trump denied an earlier ban
To keep guns from the mentally ill
And would not allow a new bill.

Accepting lobbyists' offers
Is truly ill advised
If adding to your coffers
Means risking children's lives.

The diligence we must do
Is not just passing tips.
Let's get rid of all the VIPS
Who vote "no" on gun control.

Already there have been "no" votes
On assault weapons and such.
For our country, what are our hopes
When legislators don't seem to care much?

"Boys will be boys"
May be quite true.
They play with their toys,
But what is Congress doing for you?

"A little child shall lead them."
That's what the Bible said.
But our current Congress
Would rather have guns instead.

"And a little child shall lead them."
Cheers to those kids
In Never Again MSD.
I stand with them.

Let's cheer on the kids.
They're braver than we
For calling out the NRA pawns.
The adults have been absentee.

Cheers to the kids!
They're smarter than we
And more courageous too
For not doing the NRA's bids.

The kids have got more balls
Then all of you who roam the halls.
Do your job and be wise
Before another child dies.

The mentally ill
Are those of you
Who know the gun problem
But refuse to do
Anything at all
That might disrupt
The NRA's flow of money
From it to you.

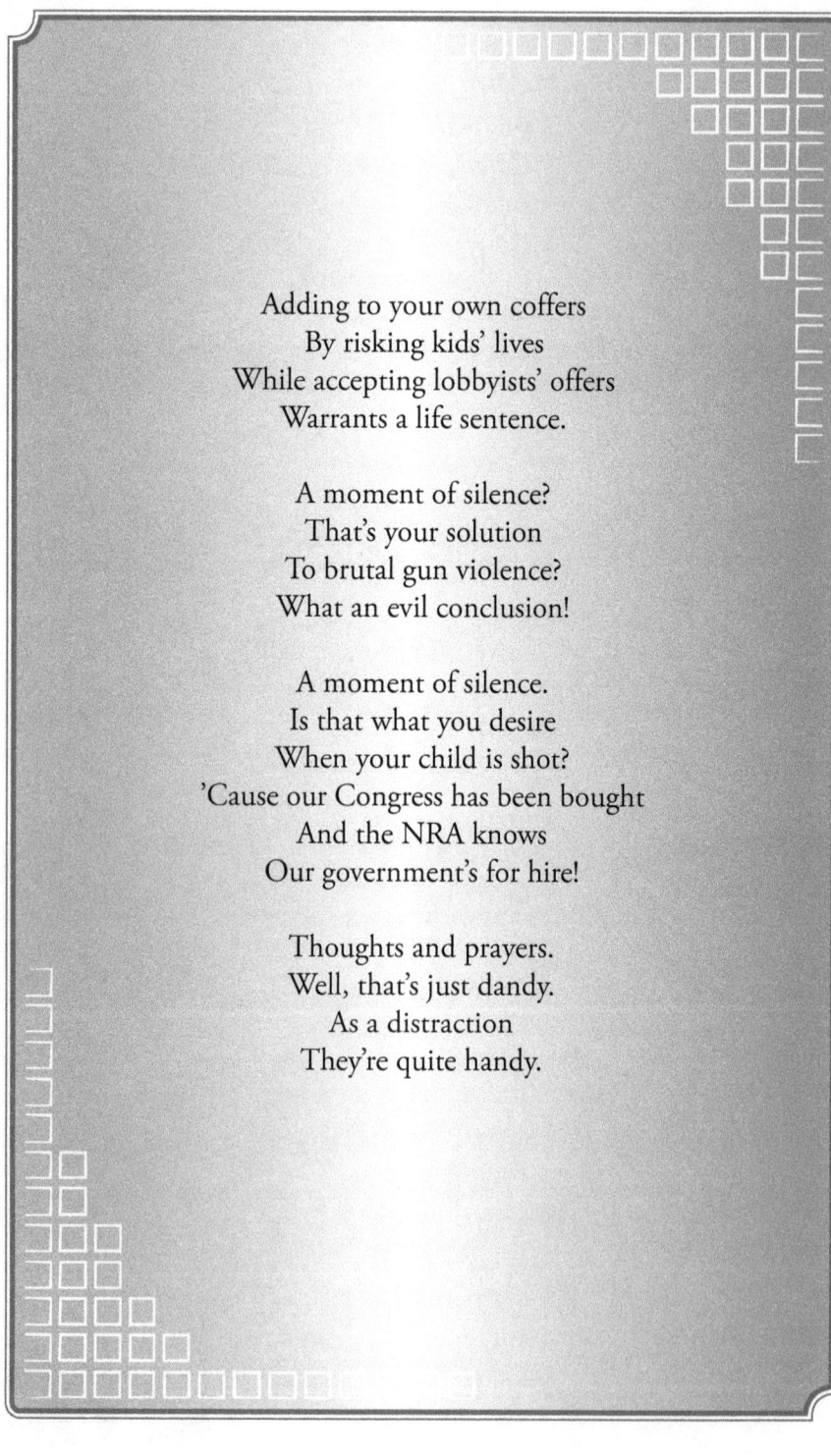

Adding to your own coffers
By risking kids' lives
While accepting lobbyists' offers
Warrants a life sentence.

A moment of silence?
That's your solution
To brutal gun violence?
What an evil conclusion!

A moment of silence.
Is that what you desire
When your child is shot?
'Cause our Congress has been bought
And the NRA knows
Our government's for hire!

Thoughts and prayers.
Well, that's just dandy.
As a distraction
They're quite handy.

What good do your
Thoughts and prayers do
If you don't give
The problem its due?

"And a little child shall lead them,"
So the Bible says.
In Parkland the children
Are now leading the way
To cutting down the NRA.

Sometimes our kids know best.
They say, "Gun control is needed,
Not just prayers and all the rest."
Maybe the kids should be in charge.
They don't work at the NRA's behest.

You've been silent enough
For Sandy Hook, Vegas, and others.
Do you all get money
For each gun sold,
Or it is just your druthers?

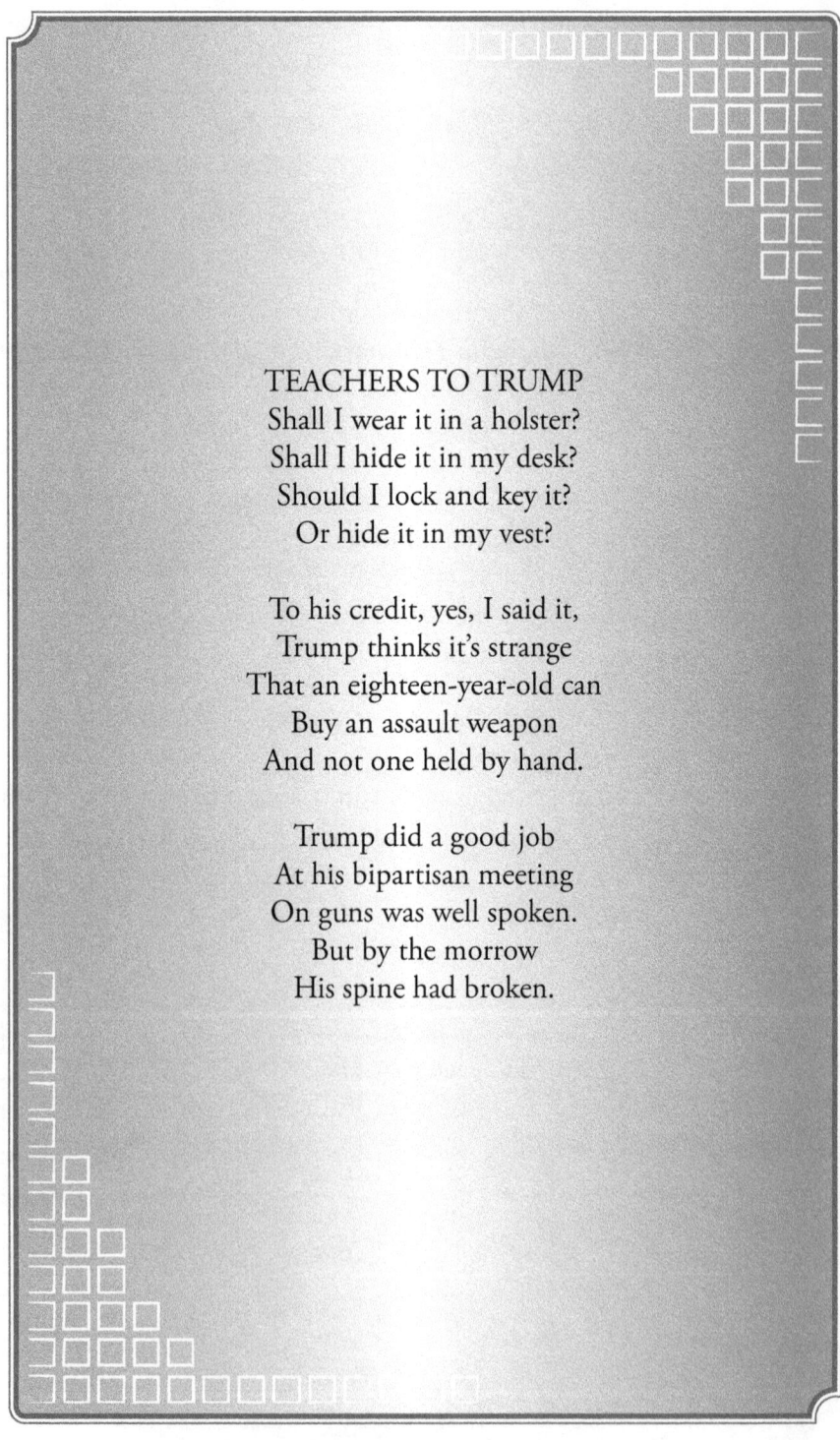

TEACHERS TO TRUMP
Shall I wear it in a holster?
Shall I hide it in my desk?
Should I lock and key it?
Or hide it in my vest?

To his credit, yes, I said it,
Trump thinks it's strange
That an eighteen-year-old can
Buy an assault weapon
And not one held by hand.

Trump did a good job
At his bipartisan meeting
On guns was well spoken.
But by the morrow
His spine had broken.

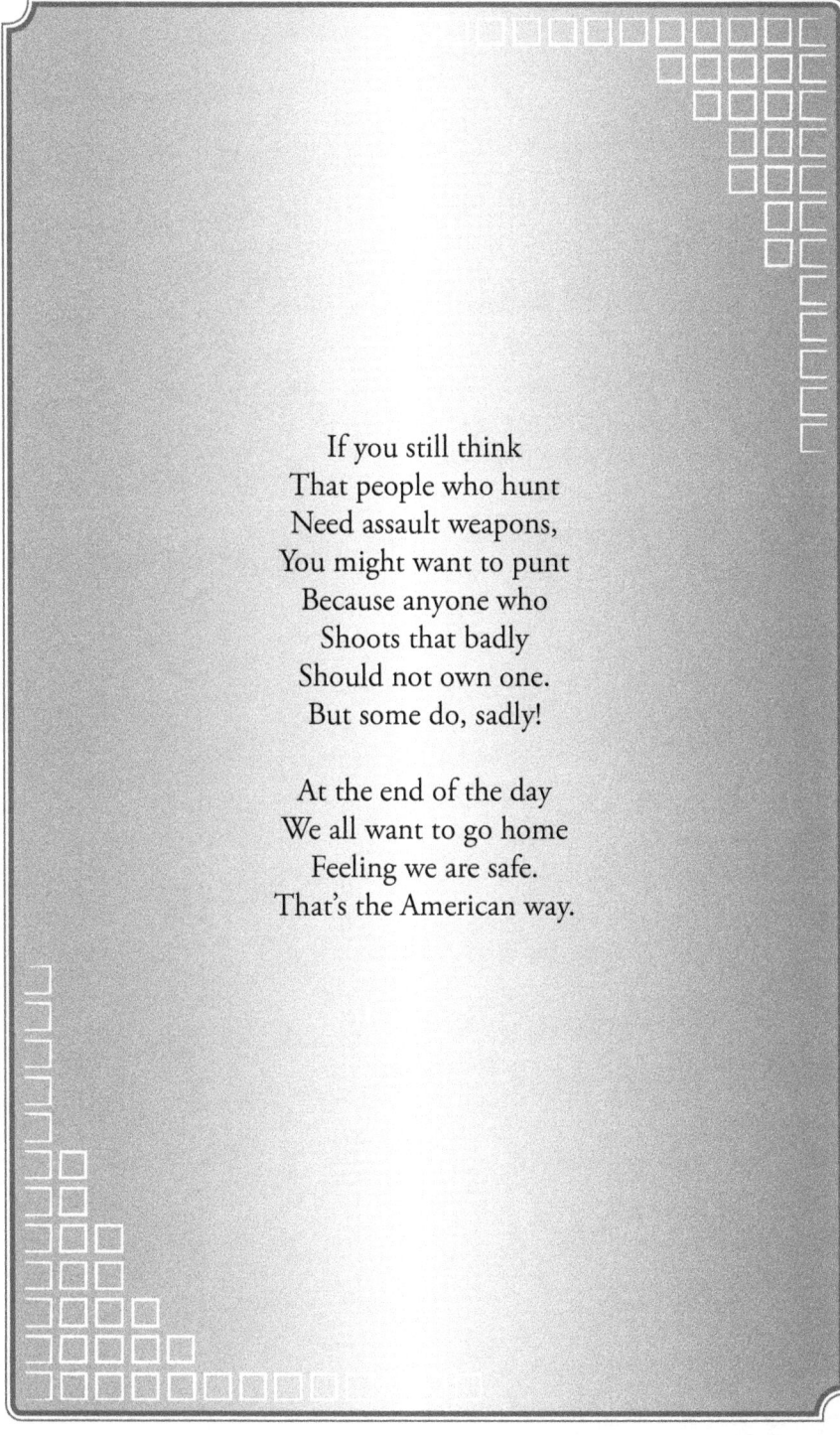

If you still think
That people who hunt
Need assault weapons,
You might want to punt
Because anyone who
Shoots that badly
Should not own one.
But some do, sadly!

At the end of the day
We all want to go home
Feeling we are safe.
That's the American way.

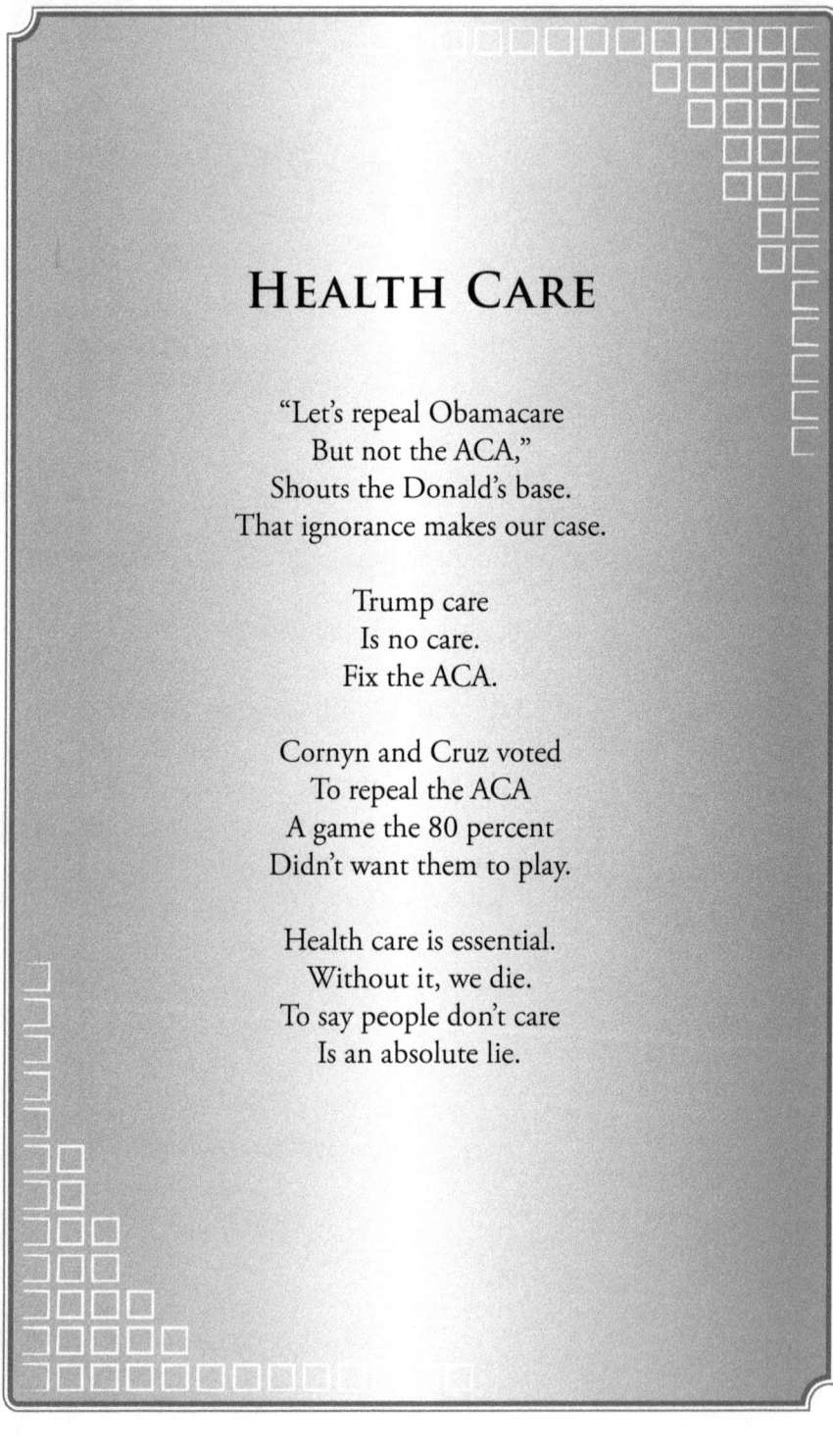

HEALTH CARE

"Let's repeal Obamacare
But not the ACA,"
Shouts the Donald's base.
That ignorance makes our case.

Trump care
Is no care.
Fix the ACA.

Cornyn and Cruz voted
To repeal the ACA
A game the 80 percent
Didn't want them to play.

Health care is essential.
Without it, we die.
To say people don't care
Is an absolute lie.

Old Mother Hubbard's
Cupboard is bare.
Medicaid's purpose?
Provide poor some fare.

Health care needs reform,
Upon my word.
But just to repeal it
Was patently absurd.

Thirteen men, white and old,
Meeting in secret
(Now isn't that bold?)
To write a bill that
Has most of us upset.

President Trump recently stated
Health care in Australia
Is better than ours
Cause ours can fail ya.

With Trump health care,
As you will discover,
Most things that befall
It will not cover.

Don't cut my Medicare.
My health that will impair.
I paid my share;
So that's not fair.
For sustainability prepare.

Health care needs correction,
But to repeal and start over
Seems more like infection.

Meals on Wheels
Seem innocuous.
To defund them
Seems obnoxious.

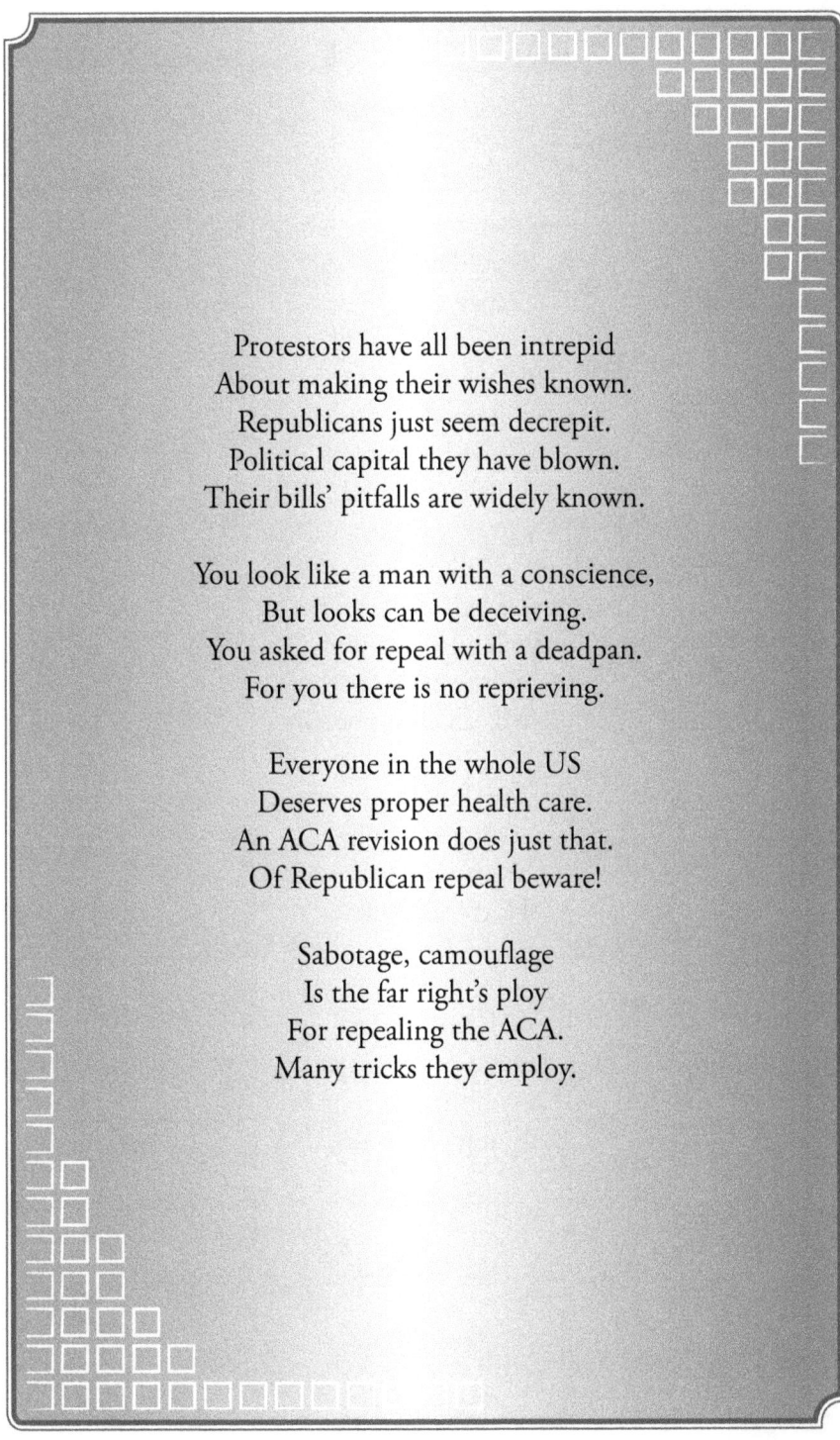

Protestors have all been intrepid
About making their wishes known.
Republicans just seem decrepit.
Political capital they have blown.
Their bills' pitfalls are widely known.

You look like a man with a conscience,
But looks can be deceiving.
You asked for repeal with a deadpan.
For you there is no reprieving.

Everyone in the whole US
Deserves proper health care.
An ACA revision does just that.
Of Republican repeal beware!

Sabotage, camouflage
Is the far right's ploy
For repealing the ACA.
Many tricks they employ.

Republican senators
(Except for three)
Voted for a bill
They wanted not to see.
Thank goodness it failed.
We've had our fill.
(It later passed.)

Moran, Collins, Paul, and Lee
Are heroes of a sort.
The final outcome we will see
And hope it's something
We can all support.

Mitch McConnell
Dodged a bullet.
If Trumpcare had won,
He'd really own it.
(It did, and he does along with Ryan.)

Republicans in the Senate
Have a cowardly side.
They didn't want the bill
But hung on for the ride.

The fact that Texas closed
Most women's clinics
Helped it win the title
"Highest maternal death rate"
Of any US state.
More ignorance exposed!

To sabotage health care,
Trump was determined.
By threatening senators
He made them rescind.

McConnell and Ryan
Keep on lyin'
About health care.
They're quite a pair.

On women's rights
Burkett's not hot.
To their plight
She listens not.

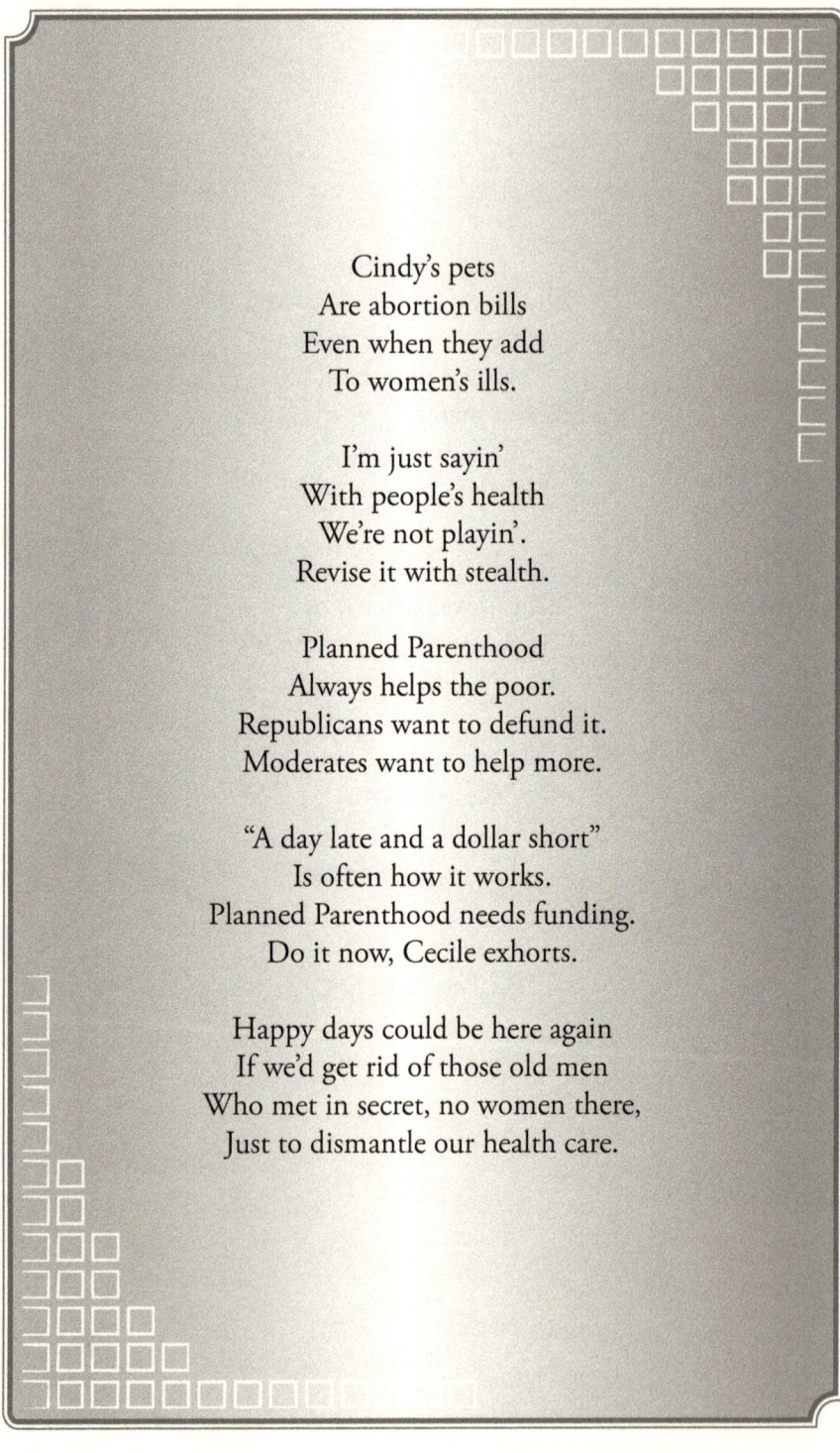

Cindy's pets
Are abortion bills
Even when they add
To women's ills.

I'm just sayin'
With people's health
We're not playin'.
Revise it with stealth.

Planned Parenthood
Always helps the poor.
Republicans want to defund it.
Moderates want to help more.

"A day late and a dollar short"
Is often how it works.
Planned Parenthood needs funding.
Do it now, Cecile exhorts.

Happy days could be here again
If we'd get rid of those old men
Who met in secret, no women there,
Just to dismantle our health care.

IMMIGRATION

Trump's third wife is an immigrant
Who immigrated from Slovenia.
So when T's on a bigoted rant
He should think closer—Melania.

The Drumpfs immigrated from Germany.
Now it's "close the gate" to many
Who are just as deserving
And not as self-serving.

Trump has the gonads
To go after all nomads.
His aversion to them is hard to see
Because the Drumpf family
And even Melania
Once were nomads, we agree.

As Trump would say,
"Many of the immigrants
Are very bad people.
Some are criminals.
Some are rapists."
Oh, wait!
Weren't the Drumpfs immigrants?

Trump wants to build a wall
To keep the undesirables out.
The only problem with this din?
The wall that walls them out
Will also wall us in.
Remember Berlin?

Trump wants to spend
Twenty billion for a wall
Most people don't want.
That takes mucho gall.

Humpty Dumpty
Wanted a wall.
Mexico wouldn't pay
So he had a good bawl.

The wall! The wall!
My country for a wall.
Mexico won't pay,
Or so they say.
I'll pretend. That's all.

A wall thirty feet high
Should do the trick
Unless the bad people
Fly over on broomsticks.

By "Make America Great Again,"
Trump seems to mean
When white men were in charge,
With no immigrants at large.

We mourn the loss of reason
In this election season.
Trump tweets every morn.
Thin skin must be the reason.

Iffen you kin talk Engleesh
Good enuf ta git aroun',
You talk as good as DJT.
You kin cum into the kuntry
Iffen you also have a skill.

The only wall
That's needed
Is the one
Between church and state.

LGBTQ

Of all the Texans obsessed with bathrooms,
Patrick seems to be the worst.
He needs to understand transgenders first
Before he makes their lives more cursed.

Cindy Burkett does not believe
In democratic traditional values.
She votes against women
And against LBTGs
Her attitude smacks of abuse.

Says a man never in the service,
"We need a strong military
But we want no transgenders."
Of him I'd be very wary.

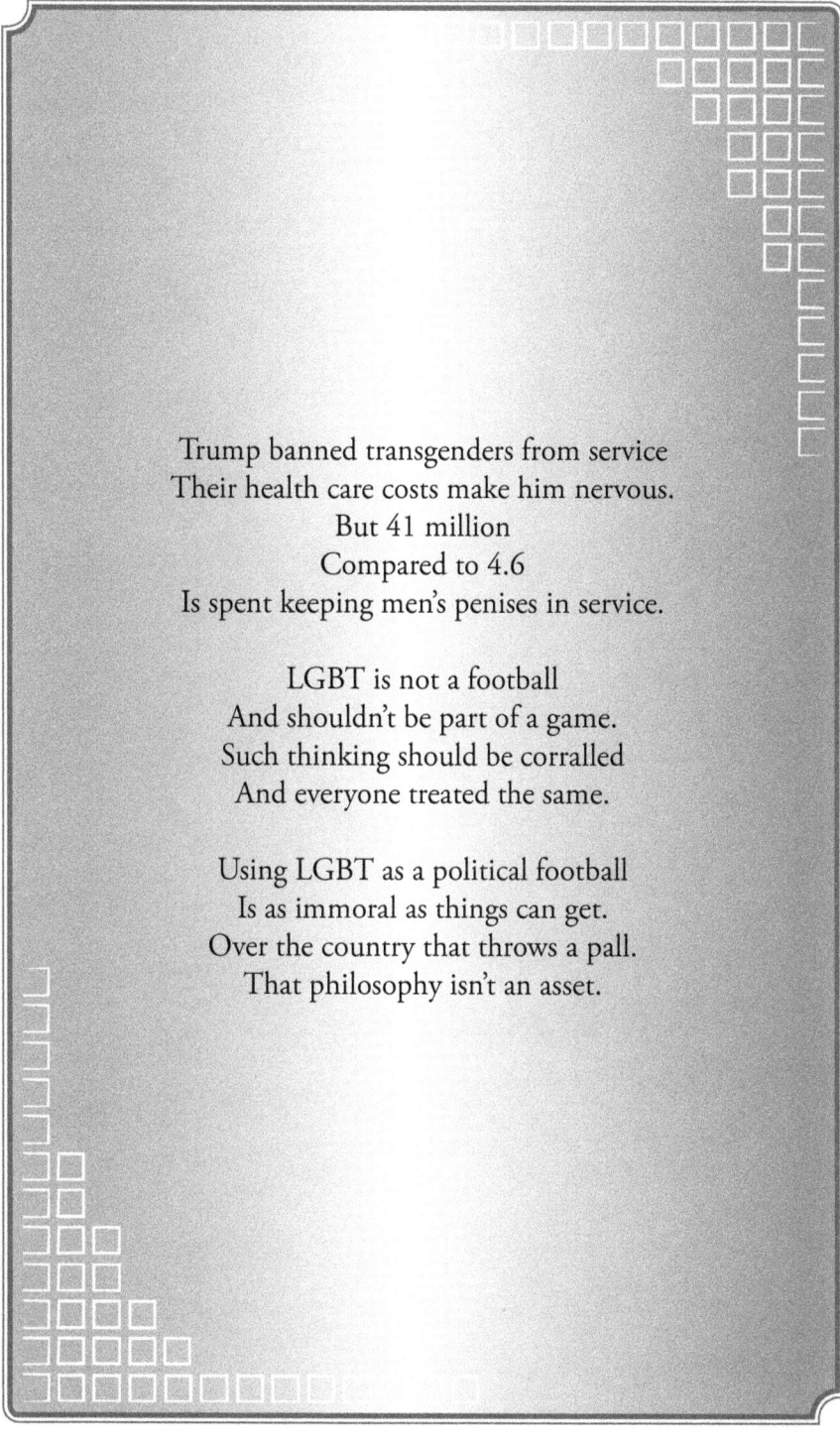

Trump banned transgenders from service
Their health care costs make him nervous.
But 41 million
Compared to 4.6
Is spent keeping men's penises in service.

LGBT is not a football
And shouldn't be part of a game.
Such thinking should be corralled
And everyone treated the same.

Using LGBT as a political football
Is as immoral as things can get.
Over the country that throws a pall.
That philosophy isn't an asset.

Russian Collusion

Trump's Russian salad
Turns out to be valid.
That T and R colluded
Can't be refuted.

Like a great big ostrich,
Trump's head's in the sand.
Neither he nor his base
Can begin to understand
The damage from passivity
When he refuses to take a stand
Regarding Russia's proclivity
To spy on our activity.
A serious reaction we demand.

Colluding with Russia
To win elections
Turns most of us off.
Here's our selection:
Anyone not a dummkopf.

Trump is a sycophant
Whose allegiance lies
Across the Atlantic
With Putin. Surprise! Surprise!

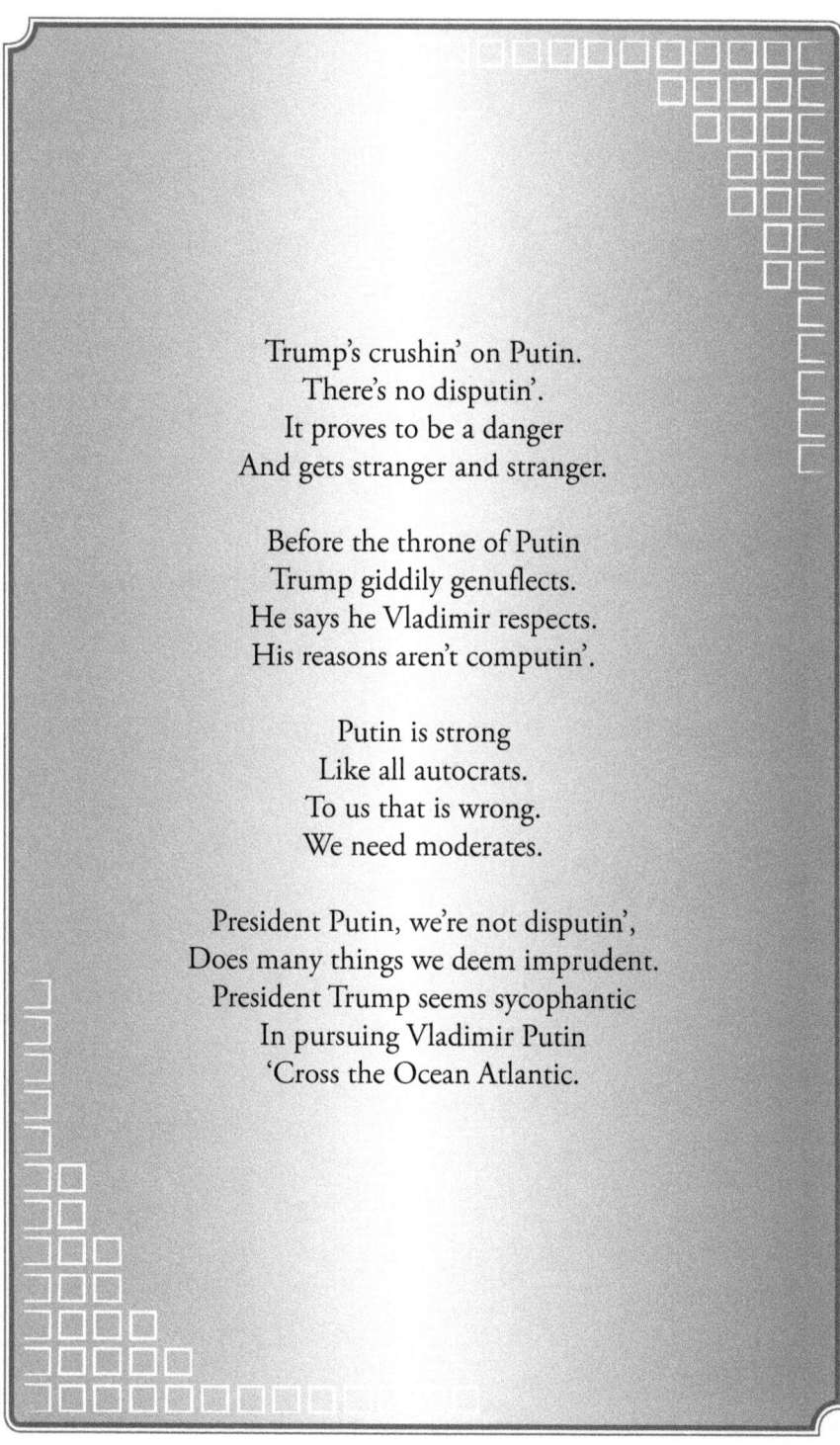

Trump's crushin' on Putin.
There's no disputin'.
It proves to be a danger
And gets stranger and stranger.

Before the throne of Putin
Trump giddily genuflects.
He says he Vladimir respects.
His reasons aren't computin'.

Putin is strong
Like all autocrats.
To us that is wrong.
We need moderates.

President Putin, we're not disputin',
Does many things we deem imprudent.
President Trump seems sycophantic
In pursuing Vladimir Putin
'Cross the Ocean Atlantic.

Putin is a master manipulator.
Trump is a suck-up twit.
Which one do you think
Will win this battle of wit?

Either Trump is dangerously gullible
And believes Phillips, Hannity and Jones,
Or Trump is deliberately lying
And thinks that buys him some stones.

Trump's susceptibility
To anything Putin
Comes from his gullibility
To flattery. No refutin'.

Collusion. Confusion.
Why do we care?
Because misconduct
Is the admin's daily fare.

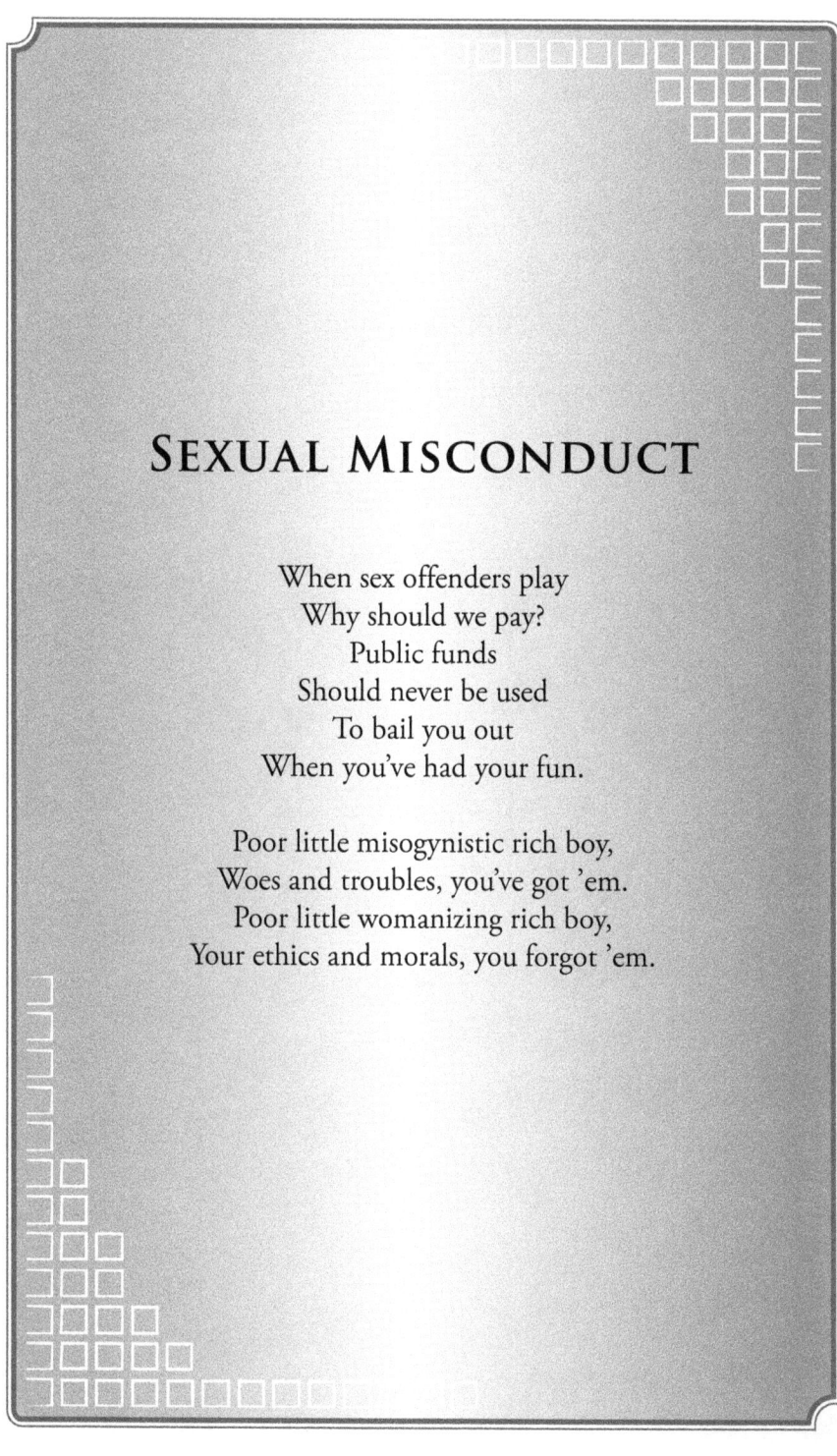

SEXUAL MISCONDUCT

When sex offenders play
Why should we pay?
Public funds
Should never be used
To bail you out
When you've had your fun.

Poor little misogynistic rich boy,
Woes and troubles, you've got 'em.
Poor little womanizing rich boy,
Your ethics and morals, you forgot 'em.

56

TEXAS STUFF

Texas is the winner
Bigger and better
Top of the heap
It claims the crown
For women's clinics closed
Now maternal deaths abound.

Transgender Bathroom Bill
Abbott and Patrick,
Two peas in a pod.
Both narrow-minded,
They like to play God.

Patrick and Abbott
Think way too much
About where people pee
And other such stuff.

Patrick and Abbott need to remove
The sticks from their asses.
On their obsessive behavior
We won't give them passes.

Patrick has an obsession
About where people pee.
So he favors a law
Nobody wants to see.

Governor Abbott
Is in for a fight.
Many are running, but
The winner may be White.

Where people pee
Is Patrick's focus.
We don't understand
All the hocus-pocus.

Some of Patrick's actions
Have been downright queer.
Let's vote him out
And put in Collier.

Mike! Mike!
He's our man.
If anyone can do it,
Collier can.

Patrick and Collier
Are not alike.
One is a piranha,
The other is a pike.

Obsessing over bathrooms
Is his bad habit.
But that's just Greg,
Our Governor Abbott.

It's time for Governor
Abbott to go.
Any good sense
He has yet to show.

Abbott is loopy
And set in his ways.
That's why we need Lupe
In the coming days.

Abbott must go!
We all know it.
Now's our chance.
Just don't blow it.

Texas Lieutenant Governor
Collier! Collier!
He's our man.
He can do better
Than Patrick can.

Those who voted for SB3
Need to get out of office.
They're too obsessed
With where we pee.

On women's rights
Burkett's not hot.
To their plight
She listens not.

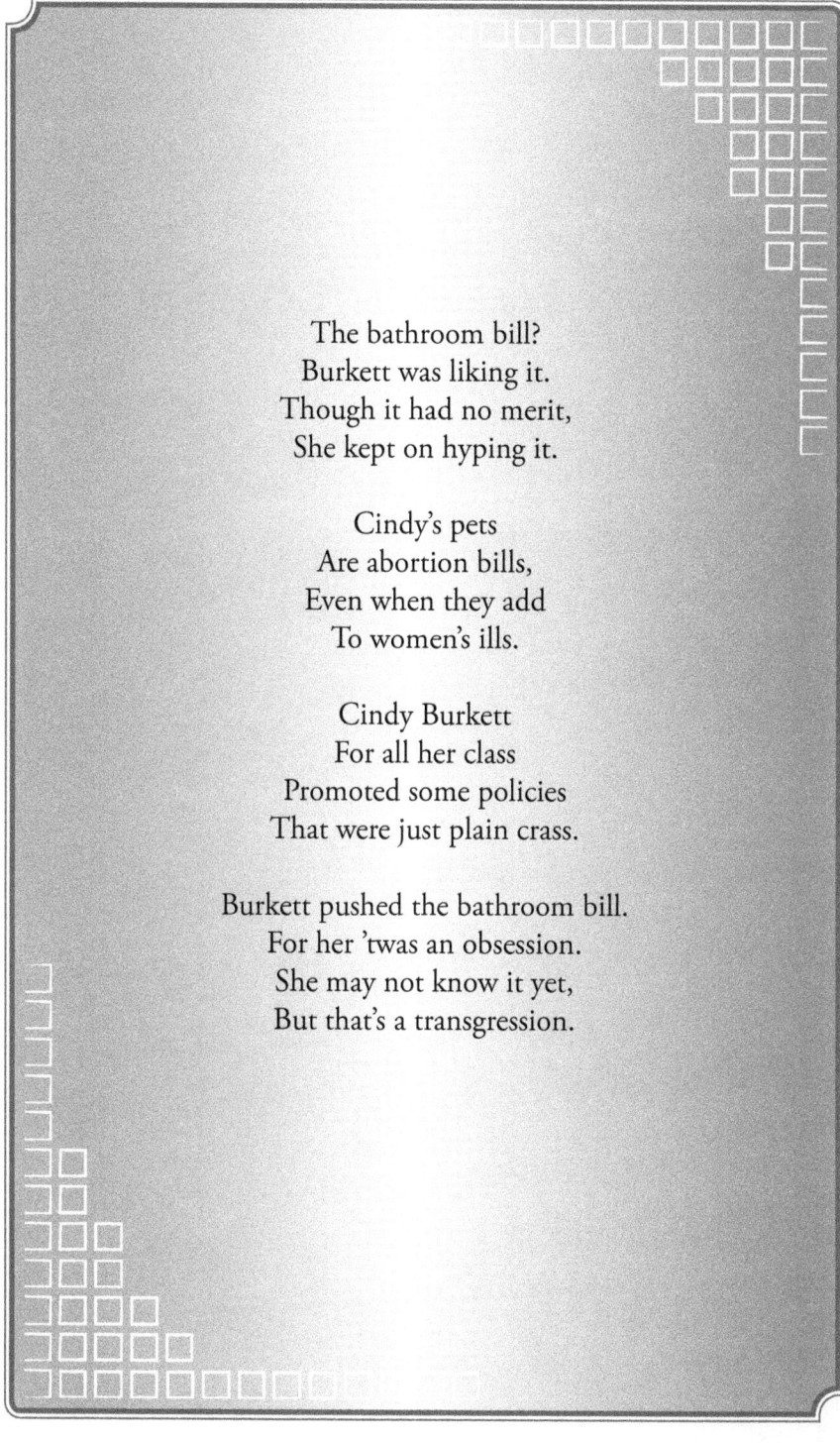

The bathroom bill?
Burkett was liking it.
Though it had no merit,
She kept on hyping it.

Cindy's pets
Are abortion bills,
Even when they add
To women's ills.

Cindy Burkett
For all her class
Promoted some policies
That were just plain crass.

Burkett pushed the bathroom bill.
For her 'twas an obsession.
She may not know it yet,
But that's a transgression.

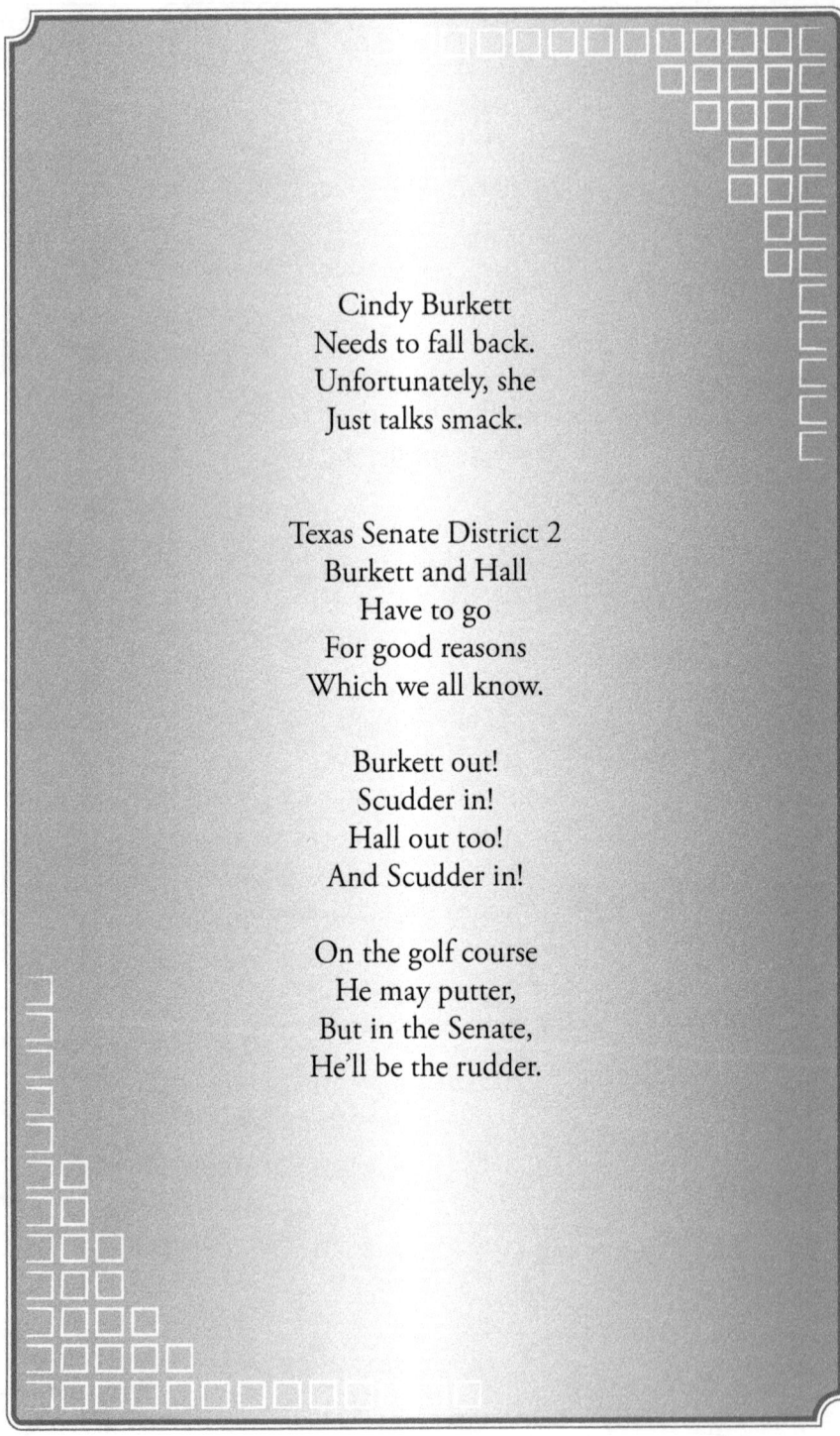

Cindy Burkett
Needs to fall back.
Unfortunately, she
Just talks smack.

Texas Senate District 2
Burkett and Hall
Have to go
For good reasons
Which we all know.

Burkett out!
Scudder in!
Hall out too!
And Scudder in!

On the golf course
He may putter,
But in the Senate,
He'll be the rudder.

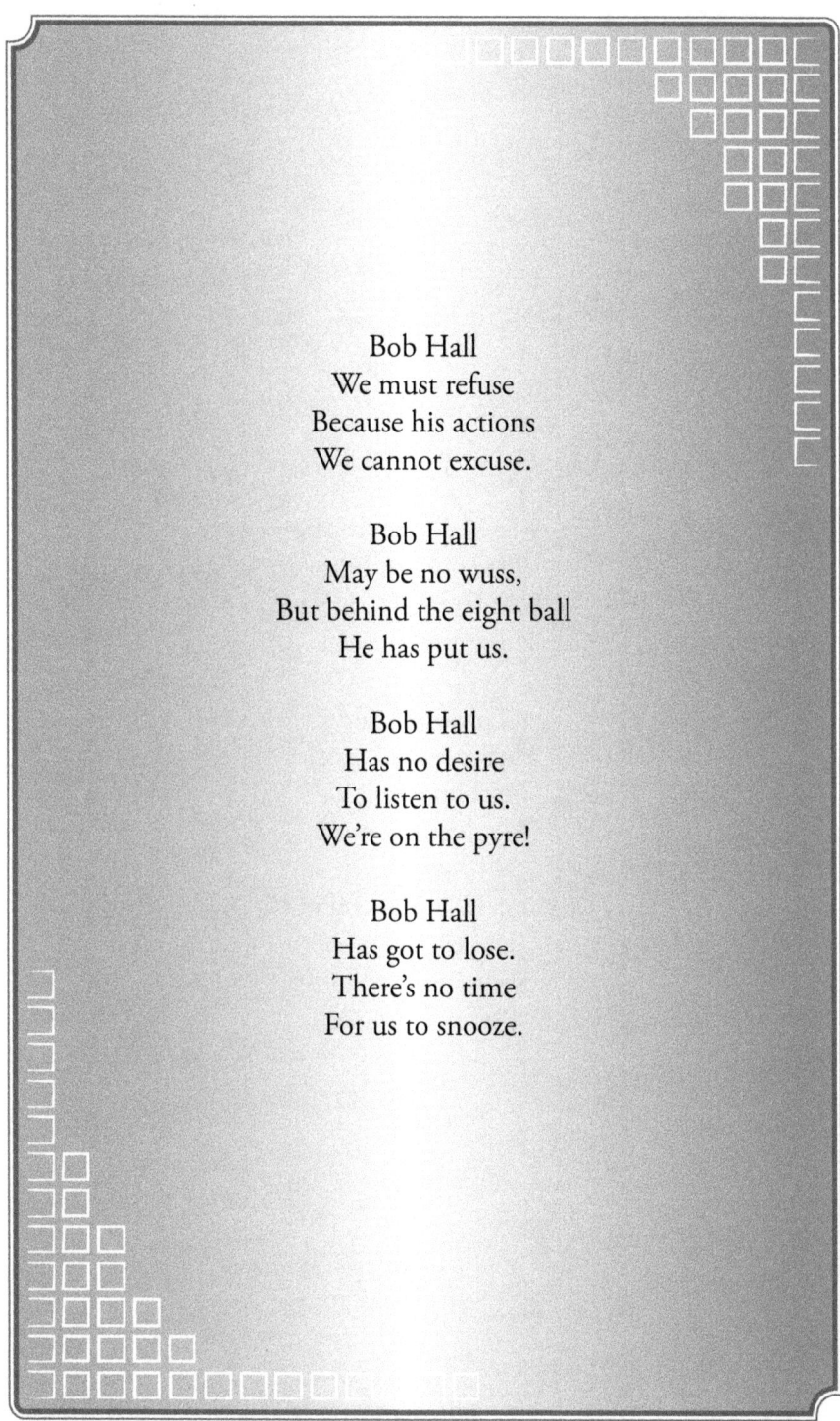

Bob Hall
We must refuse
Because his actions
We cannot excuse.

Bob Hall
May be no wuss,
But behind the eight ball
He has put us.

Bob Hall
Has no desire
To listen to us.
We're on the pyre!

Bob Hall
Has got to lose.
There's no time
For us to snooze.

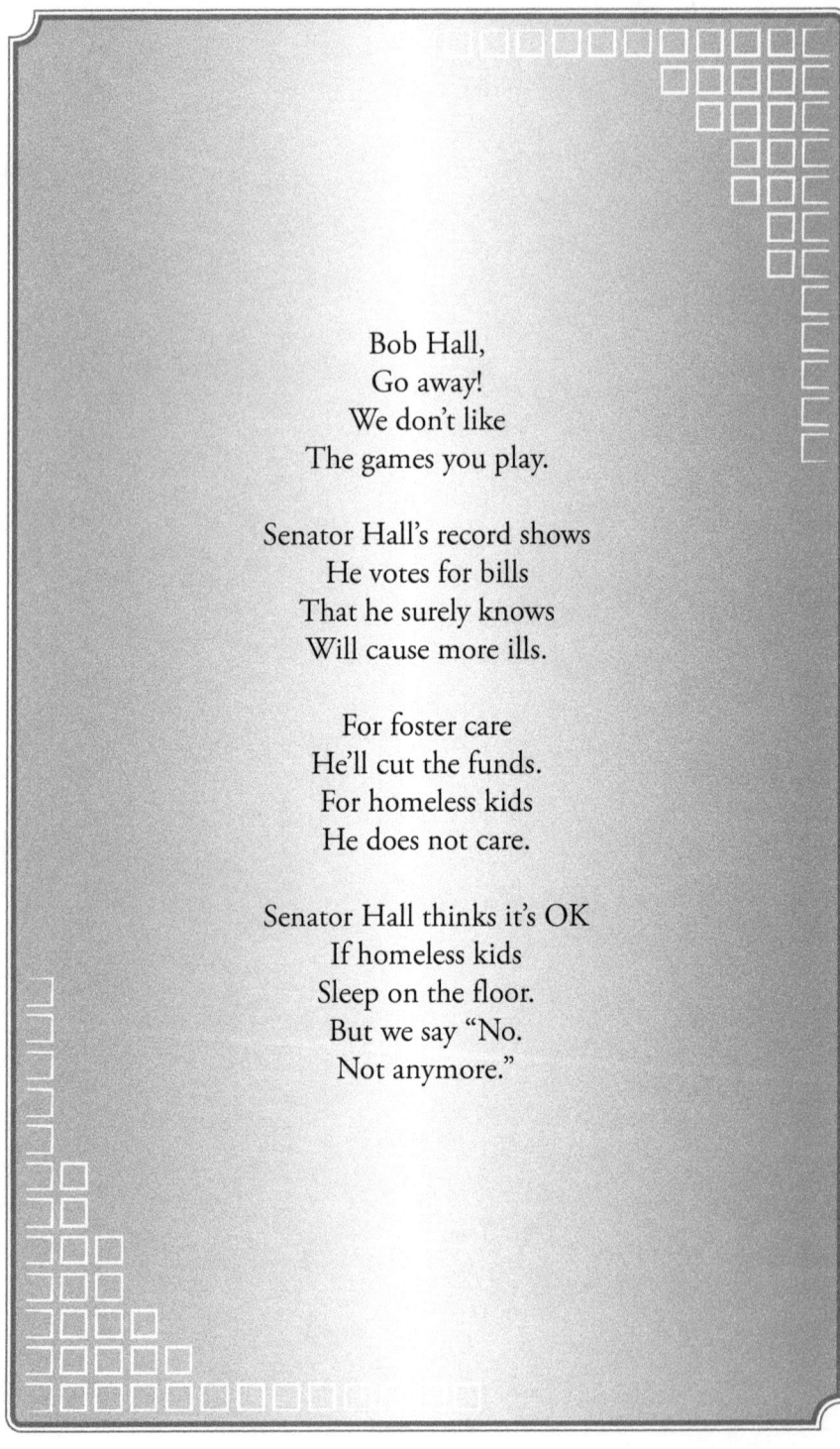

Bob Hall,
Go away!
We don't like
The games you play.

Senator Hall's record shows
He votes for bills
That he surely knows
Will cause more ills.

For foster care
He'll cut the funds.
For homeless kids
He does not care.

Senator Hall thinks it's OK
If homeless kids
Sleep on the floor.
But we say "No.
Not anymore."

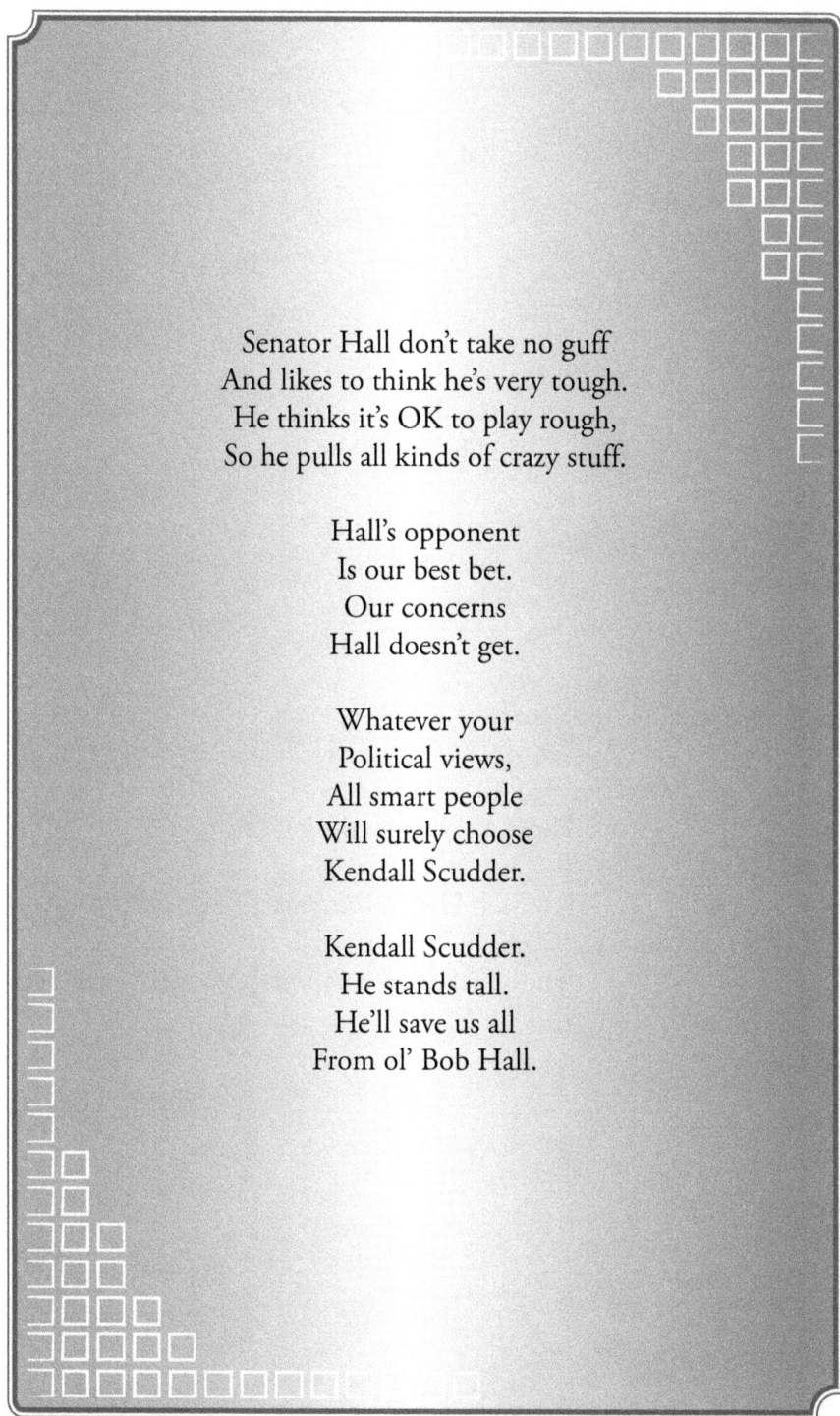

Senator Hall don't take no guff
And likes to think he's very tough.
He thinks it's OK to play rough,
So he pulls all kinds of crazy stuff.

Hall's opponent
Is our best bet.
Our concerns
Hall doesn't get.

Whatever your
Political views,
All smart people
Will surely choose
Kendall Scudder.

Kendall Scudder.
He stands tall.
He'll save us all
From ol' Bob Hall.

Scudder notably
Makes peanut butter.
Our Scudder, though,
Will help us grow.

Bread and butter.
Peanut butter
Please go vote
For Kendall Scudder.

Vote for Kendall Scudder
To replace Senator Hall.
He has a moral rudder
That'll keep us on the ball.

With Bob Hall in the Senate
We're headed for a fall.
For better representation
Vote for Scudder, Kendall.

Texas House District 33
There once was a man named Justin
Who was sitting at home just rustin'.
He decided to run
Thought 'twould be fun,
But really for power he was lustin'.

Justin Holland
Causes a din
For on the issues
He puts his own spin.

Against Justin Holland
We're taking a stand.
He doesn't act for us,
So his replacement we've planned.
Laura Gunn

Hopefully Justin Holland
Didn't run on a whim,
But on the public's wishes
He puts his own spin.

Ratcliffe, Hall, and Holland voted for SB3.
(That's the transgender bathroom bill.)
An obscene, unenforceable absurdity.
Of their obsession, we've had our fill.

US House District 4
If for Ratcliffe
You did not vote,
Of your concerns
He won't take note.

John, John. Please go away!
Don't come back another day.
We don't like the games you play
And we don't like the things you say.

Two, four, six, eight.
Who should we eliminate?
Ratcliffe. Ratcliffe.
He's always in an angry state.

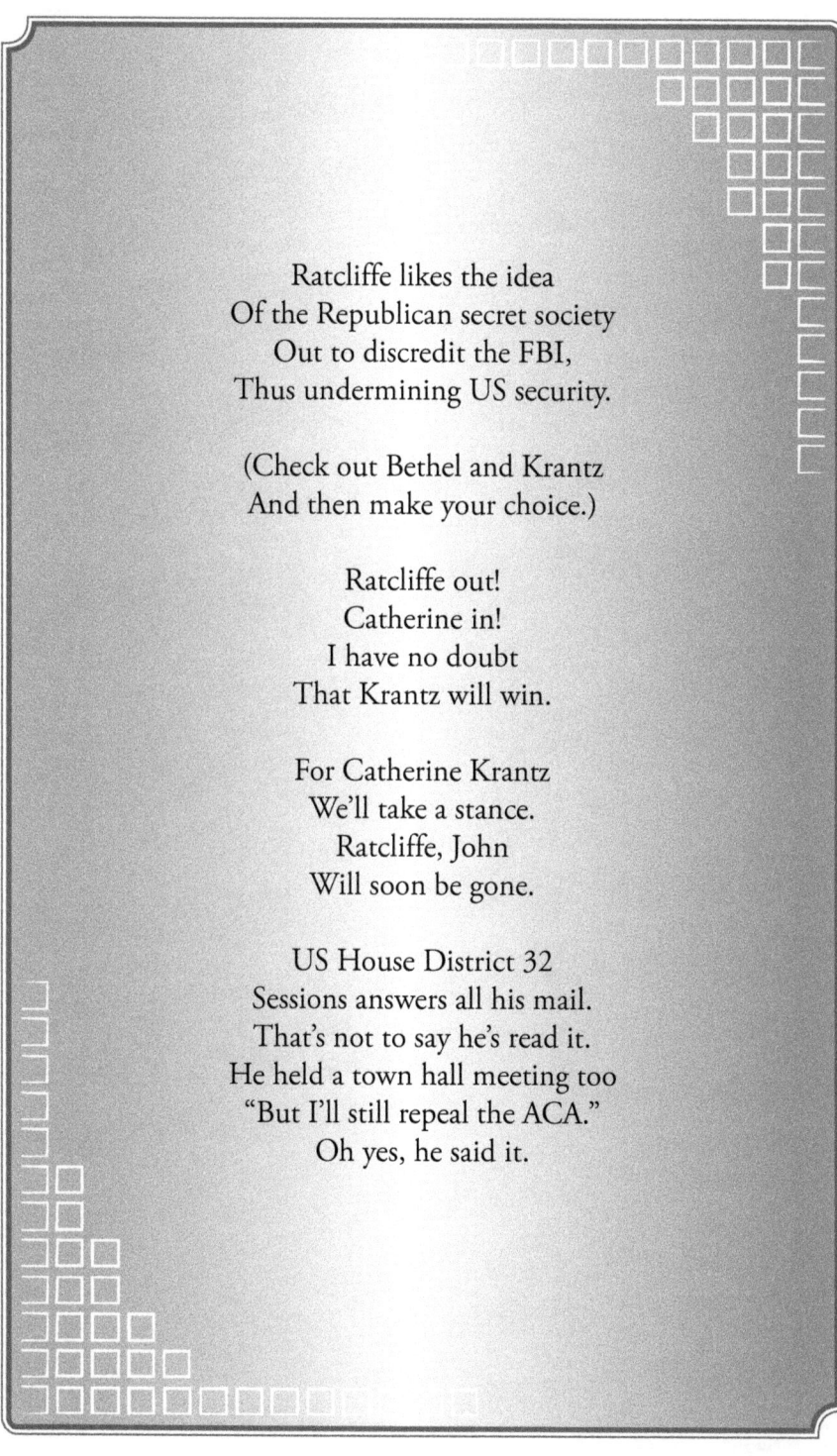

Ratcliffe likes the idea
Of the Republican secret society
Out to discredit the FBI,
Thus undermining US security.

(Check out Bethel and Krantz
And then make your choice.)

Ratcliffe out!
Catherine in!
I have no doubt
That Krantz will win.

For Catherine Krantz
We'll take a stance.
Ratcliffe, John
Will soon be gone.

US House District 32
Sessions answers all his mail.
That's not to say he's read it.
He held a town hall meeting too
"But I'll still repeal the ACA."
Oh yes, he said it.

Congressman Sessions
Has an obsession.
He voted against the ACA
And by his own confession,
Ignored all intercession.

Pete Sessions
Voted to repeal
The ACA. For real!
Not a good deal.

Pete Sessions
Has got to go
For the reasons
We all know.

Sessions. Pete Sessions.
So many obsessions
Stream out in a flood.
We need some new blood.

Allred, Meier,
And Salerno too
Would all be better
Than you know who.

(Salerno vs. Sessions)
Salerno's our choice
To get back our voice.
More qualified than most,
Though she won't boast.

Salerno fought *against* big corporations
In her quest for health care solutions.
Sessions fought *for* those same corporations
And voted down all the best solutions.

Lillian Salerno
Listens to her constituents,
Unlike Pete Sessions,
Who makes no concessions.

Elect Salerno.
Sessions we dread.
He doesn't listen.
Enough said!

Lillian Salerno
Is in my head
As our best bet.
That's what I said!

Texas House District 112
We need to unbutton
Angie Chen Button.

Button. Button.
Who's got the Button?
A gal named Brandy
Who beats even candy.

We don't need candy
(Although it's dandy).
We just need Brandy.
She'll be just grandy.

Angie Chen Button
Needs replacing.
Brandy Chambers
Is who she's facing.

Brandy! Brandy!
She's our choice
To unbutton Button
And get back our voice.

For Mayor of Rowlett
Whatever your political views
Rowlett voters
Will surely choose
Tammy Dana-Bashian.

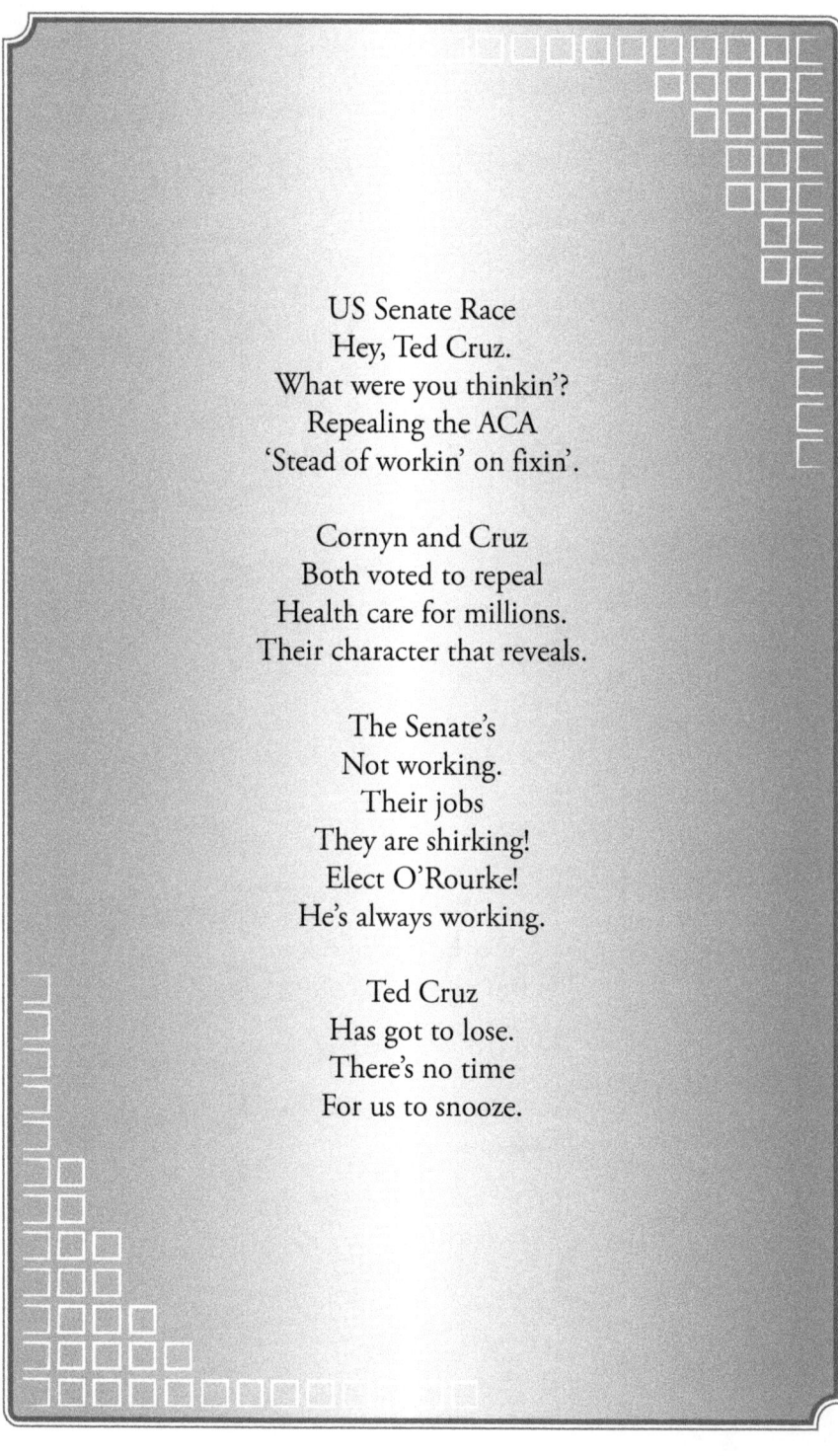

US Senate Race
Hey, Ted Cruz.
What were you thinkin'?
Repealing the ACA
'Stead of workin' on fixin'.

Cornyn and Cruz
Both voted to repeal
Health care for millions.
Their character that reveals.

The Senate's
Not working.
Their jobs
They are shirking!
Elect O'Rourke!
He's always working.

Ted Cruz
Has got to lose.
There's no time
For us to snooze.

Repeal and replace
Is a good idea.
Ted Cruz repeal
With O'Rourke replace.

Beto O'Rourke
Is an antidote
For Ted Cruz!
Get out and vote!

Your duty
Don't shirk.
Elect Beto,
Beto O'Rourke.

Ted Cruz
May be no dope,
But he's put us on
A slippery slope.

Flippity-flop! Flippity-flop!
We need someone steady.
My suggestion is O'Rourke
He's always at the ready.

Democracy
Is blowing up,
And Ted Cruz
Ignites the fuse!

Ted Cruz
We must refuse.
Most of his actions
We cannot excuse.

Ted Cruz cannot stay.
If he hollers,
Make him pay
Fifty trillion every day.

Even when Trump
Called Ted's father a killer,
Cruz kissed Trump's rump.
Oh, what a thriller!

Can a leopard change its spots?
Evidently, Cruz cannot.
For things revolting
He keeps on voting.
Our objections all come to naught.

For things revolting
Cruz and Sessions keep on voting.
Each thinks he's a big shot
But with venom, they're fraught.

Sessions huffs and puffs
And tries to blow our
Democratic house down.
But it's within our power
To elect Lillian Salerno.

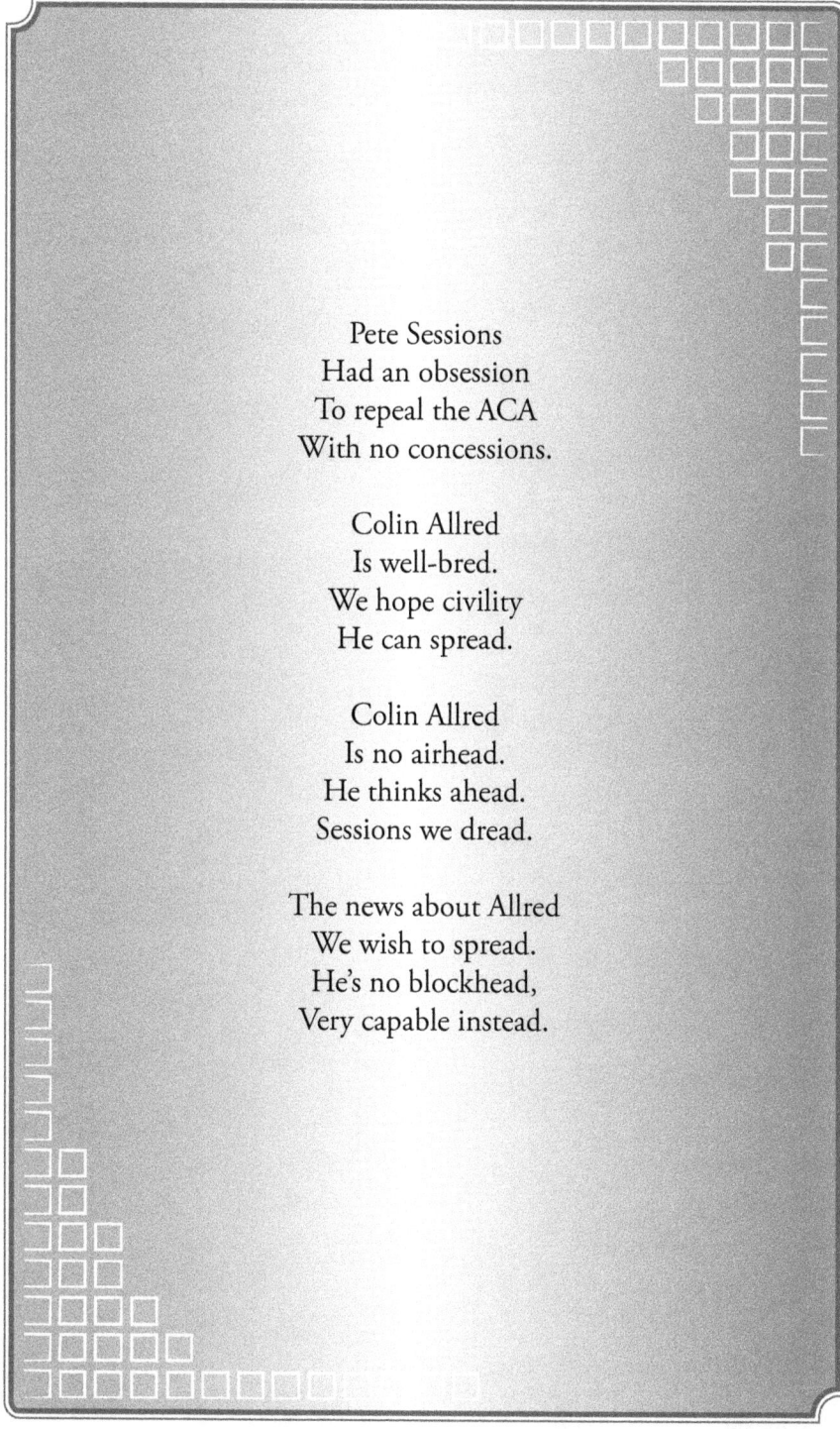

Pete Sessions
Had an obsession
To repeal the ACA
With no concessions.

Colin Allred
Is well-bred.
We hope civility
He can spread.

Colin Allred
Is no airhead.
He thinks ahead.
Sessions we dread.

The news about Allred
We wish to spread.
He's no blockhead,
Very capable instead.

George Rodriguez
Is new on the scene,
But his capability
Can already be seen.

Sessions.
Obsessions.
Repressions.
Transgressions.

Elect Salerno, Meier,
Rodriguez, or Allred
Every single one
Would move us ahead.

Most any Democrat
Would be better than Sessions,
But I think Lillian Salerno
Would meet our needs best
And is way ahead of the rest.

Hip hip hooray.
It's the big day.
Elect Lillian Salerno.
Don't let her get away!

Sessions has worked in government.
So has Lillian Salerno, and since
She cares about all her constituents,
That makes all the difference.

Cruisin' Ted
Has made his bed.
He's out of work.
Vote B. O'Rourke!

Lividity, not rigidity,
Is what senators need.
Vote for O'Rourke.
For him I do plead.

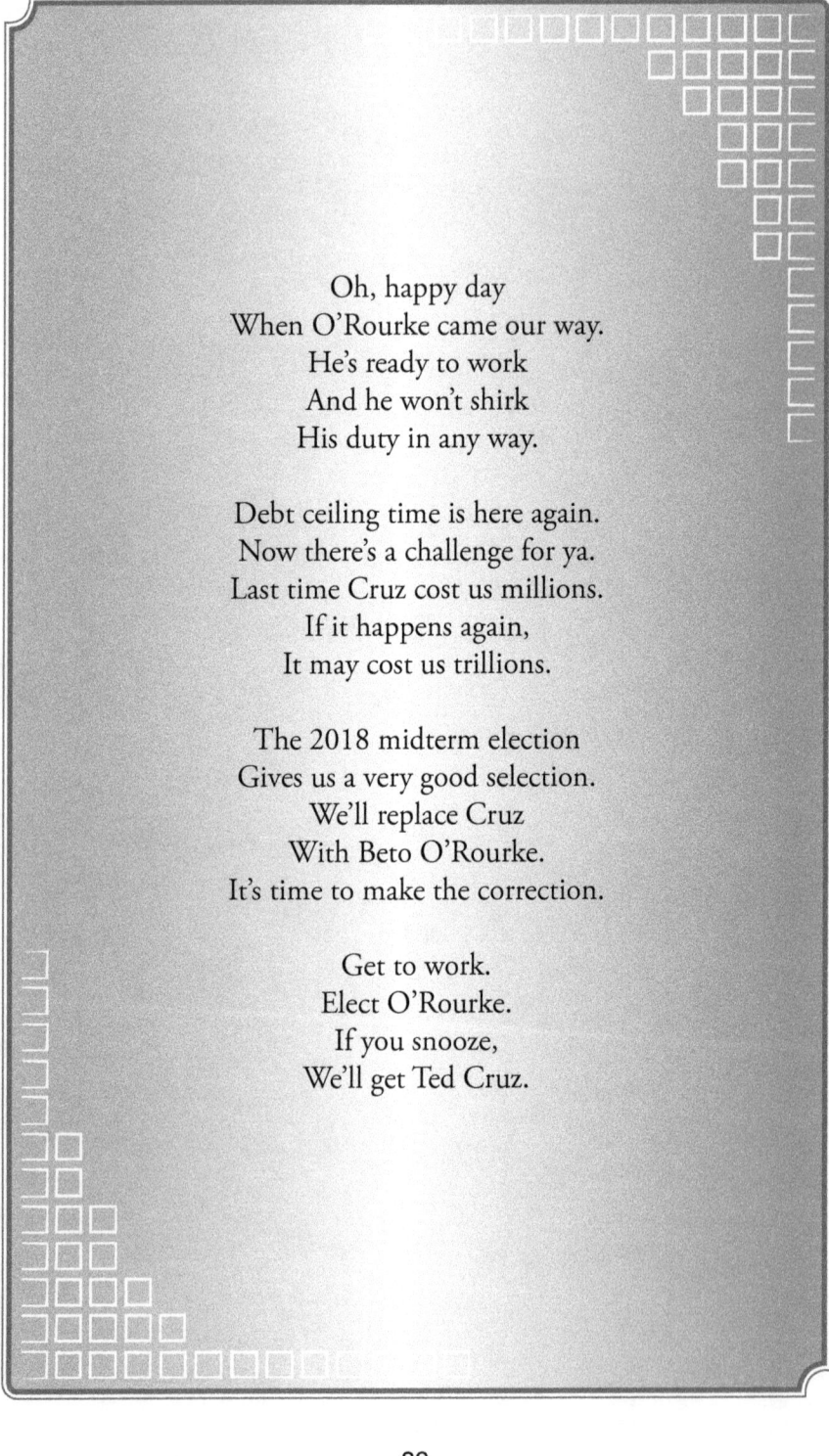

Oh, happy day
When O'Rourke came our way.
He's ready to work
And he won't shirk
His duty in any way.

Debt ceiling time is here again.
Now there's a challenge for ya.
Last time Cruz cost us millions.
If it happens again,
It may cost us trillions.

The 2018 midterm election
Gives us a very good selection.
We'll replace Cruz
With Beto O'Rourke.
It's time to make the correction.

Get to work.
Elect O'Rourke.
If you snooze,
We'll get Ted Cruz.

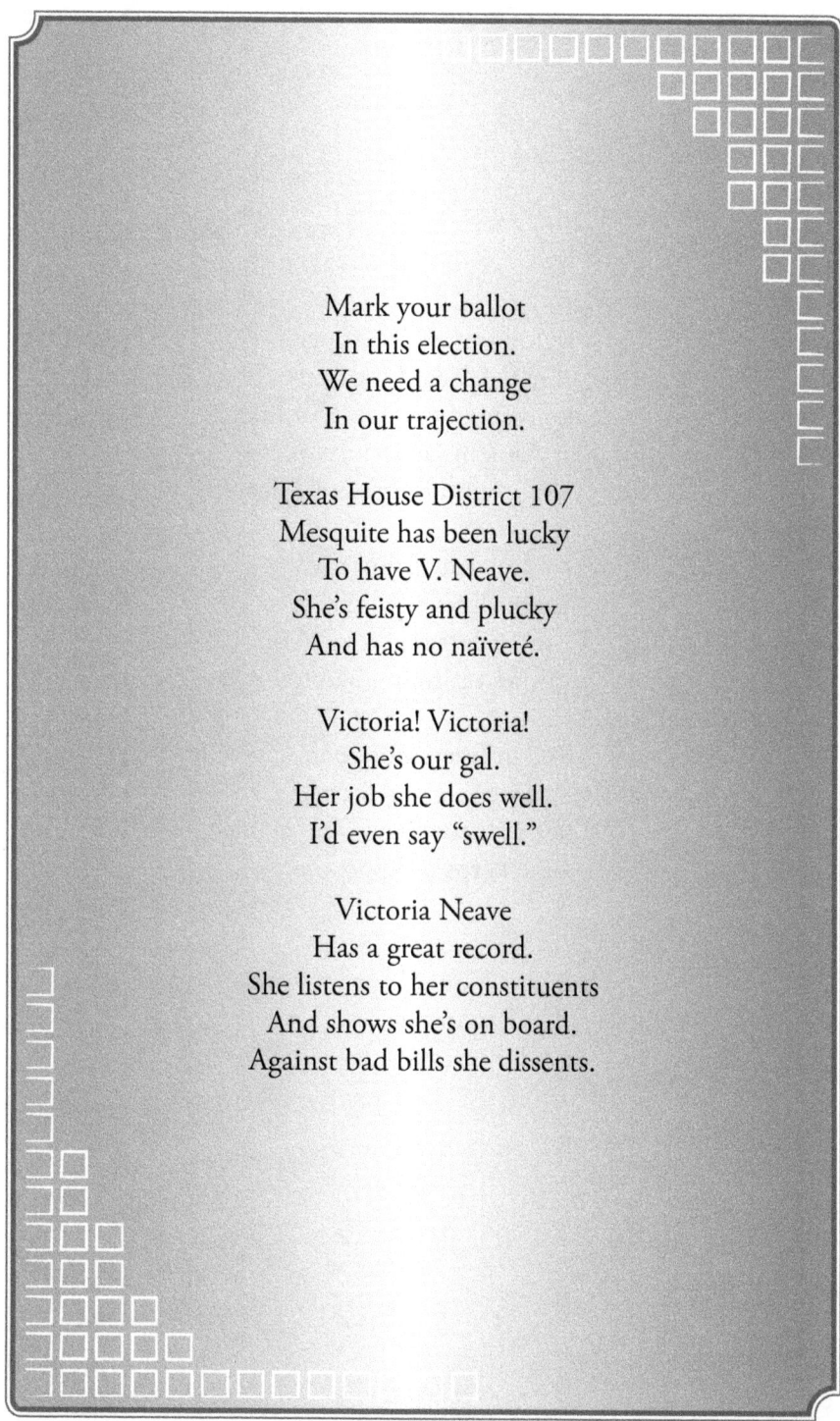

Mark your ballot
In this election.
We need a change
In our trajection.

Texas House District 107
Mesquite has been lucky
To have V. Neave.
She's feisty and plucky
And has no naïveté.

Victoria! Victoria!
She's our gal.
Her job she does well.
I'd even say "swell."

Victoria Neave
Has a great record.
She listens to her constituents
And shows she's on board.
Against bad bills she dissents.

Johnson vs. Huffines
Texas Senate District 16
Is represented by Don Huffines.
Checking his actions we glean
His voting record is definitely not fine

To what Texans say,
Huffines says "nay."
Constituents said no to SB3.
Huffines insisted it had to be.

Huffines's not good
At listening and learning.
What his constituents are saying
He keeps on spurning.

Senator Huffines
Needs to go.
Understanding of others
He does not show.

Huffines's Senate term
Will end in 2018.
Johnson will replace 'im.
On that we stand firm.

Johnson! Johnson!
We're not done
'Til Huffines we shun
And give you a run.

Nathan has capability
To beat Don Huffines
And enough ability
To perform the job.

Nathan! Nathan!
I'm a fan.
Replace Huffines.
You've a strong spine.

Texas House District 112
Chambers is ours.
We need her ambition.
As one of our stars
She works with precision.

Angie Chen Button
Has to go.
Elect Brandy Chambers
So our state can grow.

Texas House District 113
Rhetta Bowers
Never cowers.
She won't shirk
Doing her work.

Flowers to Bowers
For her stance
On gerrymandering.
We're tired of that dance!

Don't bring candy.
Don't bring flowers.
Just go vote
For Rhetta Bowers.

Rhetta Bowers
Has some powers
That our state needs
For us to succeed.

Rhetta.
We gotta getta
To make things mo' betta.
On her we should betta.

Rhetta! Rhetta!
We gotta getta.
She's our best betta
To have no regretta.

So many bills proposed in Texas
Have been remarkably silly.
I'd like some rational reps elected.
In fact, I'd be fine with Billy.

Who has the powers
To do the job right?
Rhetta Andrews Bowers
Will help fix our plight.

US House District 3
Clickety-clack.
Don't look back.
Medrick Yhap
Will take no flack.

Instead of Frick and Frack
Let's elect Medrick Yhap.
We don't want a quack
Let's throw Taylor back.

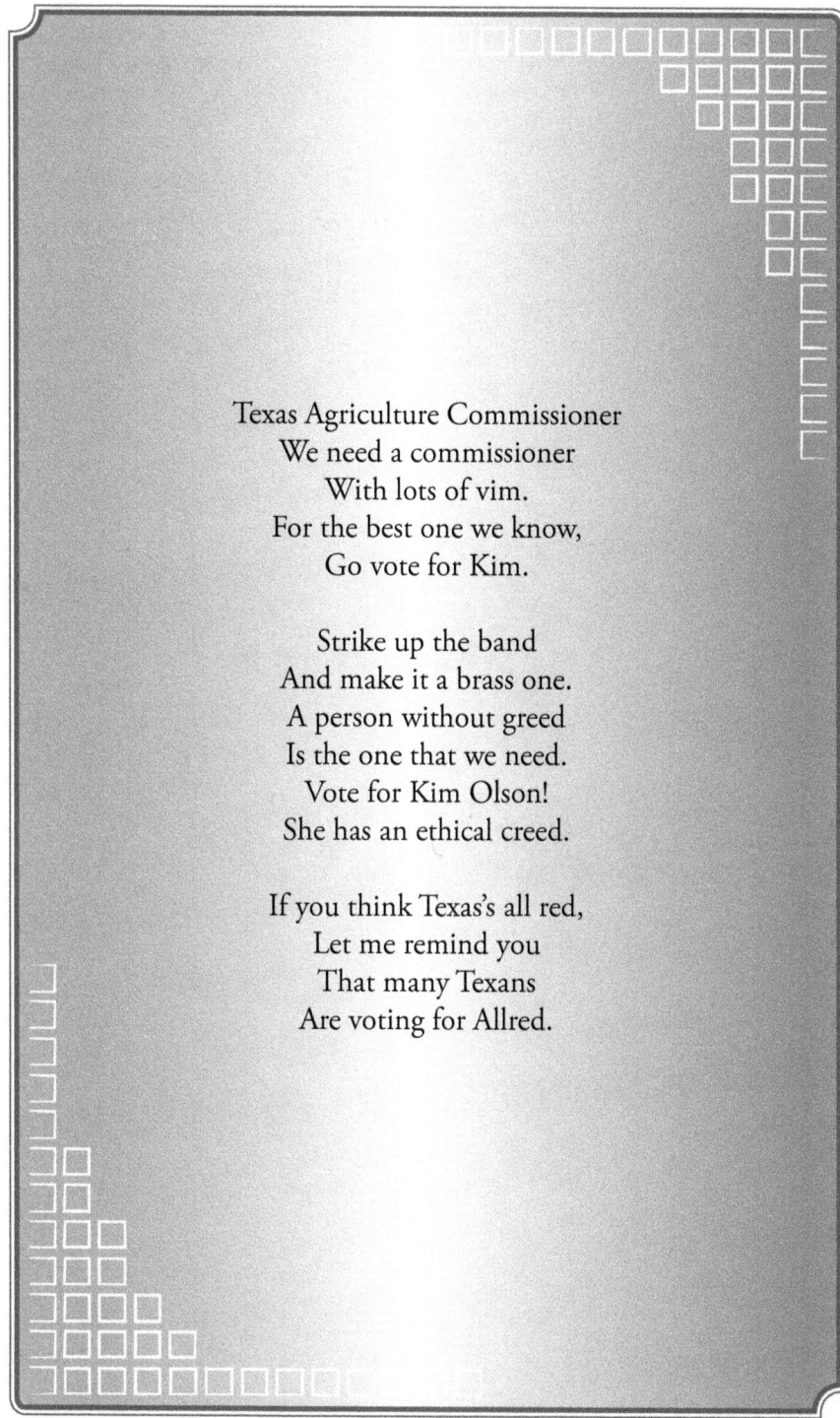

Texas Agriculture Commissioner
We need a commissioner
With lots of vim.
For the best one we know,
Go vote for Kim.

Strike up the band
And make it a brass one.
A person without greed
Is the one that we need.
Vote for Kim Olson!
She has an ethical creed.

If you think Texas's all red,
Let me remind you
That many Texans
Are voting for Allred.

Trump Presidency

There once was a man named Trump
Whose grandfather changed his name from Drumpf.
He became prez 45
And the country, no jive,
Fell down in a slump on its rump.

There once was a man named Trump
Whose country he put in a slump.
With a big ego and vain
He caused so much pain
The US fell down and went bump.

The Pied Piper of 2016
Was a crass, bigoted liar.
People followed him mindlessly.
Now the country's on fire.

Naked through the streets he walks,
Beaming as he goes
Because he's blissfully unaware
Of what everyone else knows.

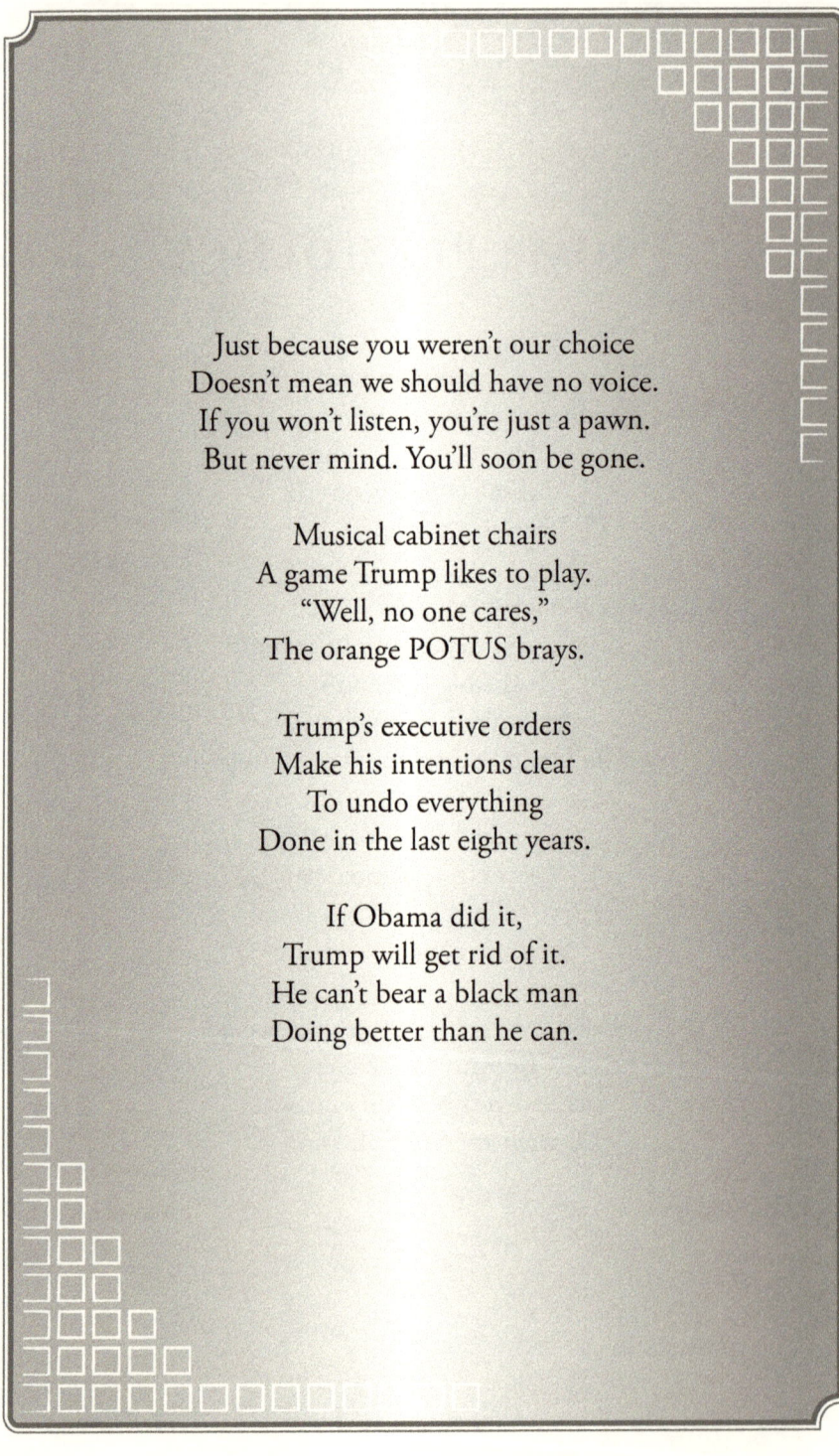

Just because you weren't our choice
Doesn't mean we should have no voice.
If you won't listen, you're just a pawn.
But never mind. You'll soon be gone.

Musical cabinet chairs
A game Trump likes to play.
"Well, no one cares,"
The orange POTUS brays.

Trump's executive orders
Make his intentions clear
To undo everything
Done in the last eight years.

If Obama did it,
Trump will get rid of it.
He can't bear a black man
Doing better than he can.

Obama ranks number 12
Among presidents, dead or alive.
Trump, so far, is below 45.
Unless he gets infinitely smarter,
He'll have to work much harder.

Whatever T's game
He's not to blame.
That honor goes
To anyone he can frame.

Trump's strategies destroy.
Resistance we must employ.
The plans he proposes
His ignorance exposes.
All we can say is "Oh boy!"

Bad decisions Trump is amassing.
His ignorance is encompassing.
He runs roughshod
Both here and abroad
Over everything good that's been passing.

The Trump admin is such a pain
From tearing our hair
We must refrain.
He acts without thinking
Our ship he is sinking.
I fear it will burst into flame.

Trump called the White House a dump.
That's talking out of his rump.
There's history galore
On every floor.
So to him we all say, "Harrumph."

The White House is the People's House
With a beautiful relevance to history.
It houses statues and artifacts
And paintings and photographs.
Trump's calling it a dump is a mystery.

The prez's style of governing
Is beyond all understanding.
The position he takes today
Tomorrow will face another way.

Trump takes pride
In cutting taxes for the rich
And benefits for the poor.
His philosophy's a bitch.

On help for the poor
He shuts the door.
On perks for the rich
He'll do even more.

Trump's given to verbosity
On a little thing called Twitter.
He cares nothing about accuracy.
Away the truth he doth fritter.

His vitriol wafts far and near
Like Nagasaki's nuclear cloud
Poisoning our democratic atmosphere.
Of our president we are not proud.

Trump has a fit of pique
And like a teenager starts to tweet
Whenever people begin to seek
The truth about his lying streak.

So loose is Trump's tongue
Our hands we have wrung.
He just sounds unstrung.
When his words are far-flung.
In his head a leak has been sprung.

Trump's tongue is so loose
It turns us bright puce.
His pulpit misuse
And language abuse
Make us long for a truce.
Or
Make us chant, "Silly goose."

Our conspiracy theorist in chief
Keeps making them up to tweet.
A psychological purge?
Or just a twittering urge?

Evidently, Trump didn't learn from Christie.
He seems to have that all twisty.
Punishing residents because of their leader
Seems like the act of a bottom-feeder.

It's quite amazing
How one so incompetent
Is so delusional
He thinks he's omnipotent.

Nothing's new under the sun.
While Trump's having fun
Nothing's getting done.
That puts us all under the gun.

Trump's money
Must be very clean.
It's been laundered enough,
Or so it would seem.

"Let's investigate Hillary,"
Says King of Distraction, Trump.
"My ratings are in a slump.
Let's try again to pillory Hillary."

If Hillary didn't have so much class,
She should pull Trump up short
On his conspiracy theories
Instead of giving him a pass.

"Lock her up," chanted Trump
In reference to Hillary.
For him to reveal things classified
He thinks is justified.

If you call him up,
Trump will reveal
Things classified
And say, "No big deal."

Donald isn't nimble
And Donald isn't quick.
He can't jump over
Mueller's candlestick.

"Lyin' Ted," said Donald J.,
"Just cannot be trusted."
But it's Trump's nose
That's growin'. He's busted!

T's tongue is so forked
It sounds like he's torqued.
His language was crude
When vitriol he spewed.
Guess his bottle's uncorked.

Every dictator
Stifles the press.
It seems our Trumptator
Won't settle for less.

Why Trump wants to muzzle
The press should be a puzzle.
But that's what dictators do
And our Trumptator does too.

Trump's ego is showing.
His nose keeps on growing
His ignorance is astounding
With dumb acts abounding.

The prez refuses to learn!
Most knowledge he doth spurn.
He just keeps on twittering
His early morning blithering.

Trump speaks impulsively
Without a thought in his head
About possible consequences
For what he has said.

Trump and his ego
Are quite a pair.
The hubris ensuing
Is our daily fare.

My kingship I'll flaunt.
I can do what I want.
My supporters won't care.
My opponents won't dare
To oppose me, I swear.

Macho, macho, macho man.
Trump thinks he's a macho man.
Actually, he's more like Peter Pan,
A little boy in fantasy land.

Obsession's a perfume for females,
But Trump uses his on his tweet mail.
He thinks it's presidential
And feels existential.
His obsessions are beyond the pale.

Berate the Donald
With something derogatory
And he'll threaten to send
You to purgatory.

Hallelujah! I don't care
What crimes I commit
'Cause a pardon is there
Waiting for me to submit.

By pardoning Joe,
Trump says loud and clear,
"If you break the law,
You need not fear."

One can only
Be pardoned
For an actual crime.
Why seek a pardon
At this early time?

Our president is ruining
Our image abroad.
Behaving obnoxiously
Brands him a fraud.

Now he wants a military parade
To show off our military power.
But that really is just a charade.
True power doesn't need a parade.

Since Trump rarely reads
His president's daily briefings,
How unprepared he must be
In case of catastrophes.

His Twitter finger
Is poised at the ready.
Anytime he feels insulted,
His stream of vitriol is steady.

Putin is hurrying
To cover their tracks.
The main thing
Is hiding their hacks.

Trump's ego and vanity
Border on insanity.
He does things erratical
And is so emphatical
He endangers all of humanity.

Our prez, a narcissist,
Keeps changing his story
To anything that
Will bring him glory.

Oh, woe is me.
It's so unfair
To do to me
What I've done to you.

Oh, boo-hoo. Yes, it's true.
I become a shrew
When you do to me
What I've done to you.

Poor little boy president
Thinks everyone's agin him.
Even with his millions
He says the system's rigged agin him.

Born into wealth
Trump had a head start.
But he thinks he made it all
By being "stable and smart."

Like Li'l Jack Horner,
Trump sticks in his thumb,
Pulls out a plum,
And says, "What a good boy am I."

Trump has so fanned the flame of fear
That most countries far and near
Find our president so scary
They have become wary
Of Americans who no visas carry.

The Donald's a strange little fellow.
In public he sometimes is mellow.
In secret he fumes
As bad bills he exhumes.
He's even been known to bellow.

Boy Scouts listening to Trump
Got an earful and a pat on the rump.
"It's OK, boys, to disrespect
Women. No need to be circumspect."
The leaders had to say sorry for T's dung dump.

When Trump starts spouting
The vitriol he is touting,
Some organizations prosper
Adding names to their roster
Because of the policies he's flouting.

"It's a disgrace what's happening
In our country."
We agree, Mr. Trump. We
Certainly do.
And according to all the punditry,
Most of it has been caused by you.

Trump, the reality TV guy,
Enjoys saying, "You're fired."
As prez, he shouldn't have been hired,
But now let's echo, "You're fired!"

Let us contemplate
Why Trump perpetuates
The theory that we would be
Better off with one who dictates.

Hey, diddle, diddle.
Trump and his fiddle.
The country is burning.
No hand is he turning
To solve any part of the riddle.

The emoluments clause
Is there for a reason.
Putting self before country
A form of treason?

Trump's cabinet members
All seem to've been picked
For their intentions to restrict
The agencies they'll dismember.

Getting in bed
With gov't corruption
Seems to be a
Republican fucktion.

Those officials who
Are involved in collusion
Leave all but a few
Filled with confusion.

Ryan and McConnell
Deserve a lot of credit
For crippling our democracy.
OK. There, I said it.

Trump alone could not have had
Such a negative effect
Without their complicity.
Both do genuflect.

Freud described our president
When narcissism defining.
He exaggerates his talent
And admiration he's expecting.

The narcissistic personality
Fits our president to a T.
He has a fragile self-esteem
But says he's the greatest
President that ever will be.

Trump and Blanche Devereaux
Have needs all the same.
To be the center of attention
That's how they play the game.

Trump can dish it
But can't take it.
He really feels burned
When the tables are turned.

Poor little boy president
Thinks everyone's pickin' on him.
Even with all his millions
Says the system's rigged agin him.

The prez keeps adding
More crimes to his repertoire.
Wherever he's gadding,
He garners some more.

Trump won't own
Anything bad.
He just shifts the blame
To that Obama cad.

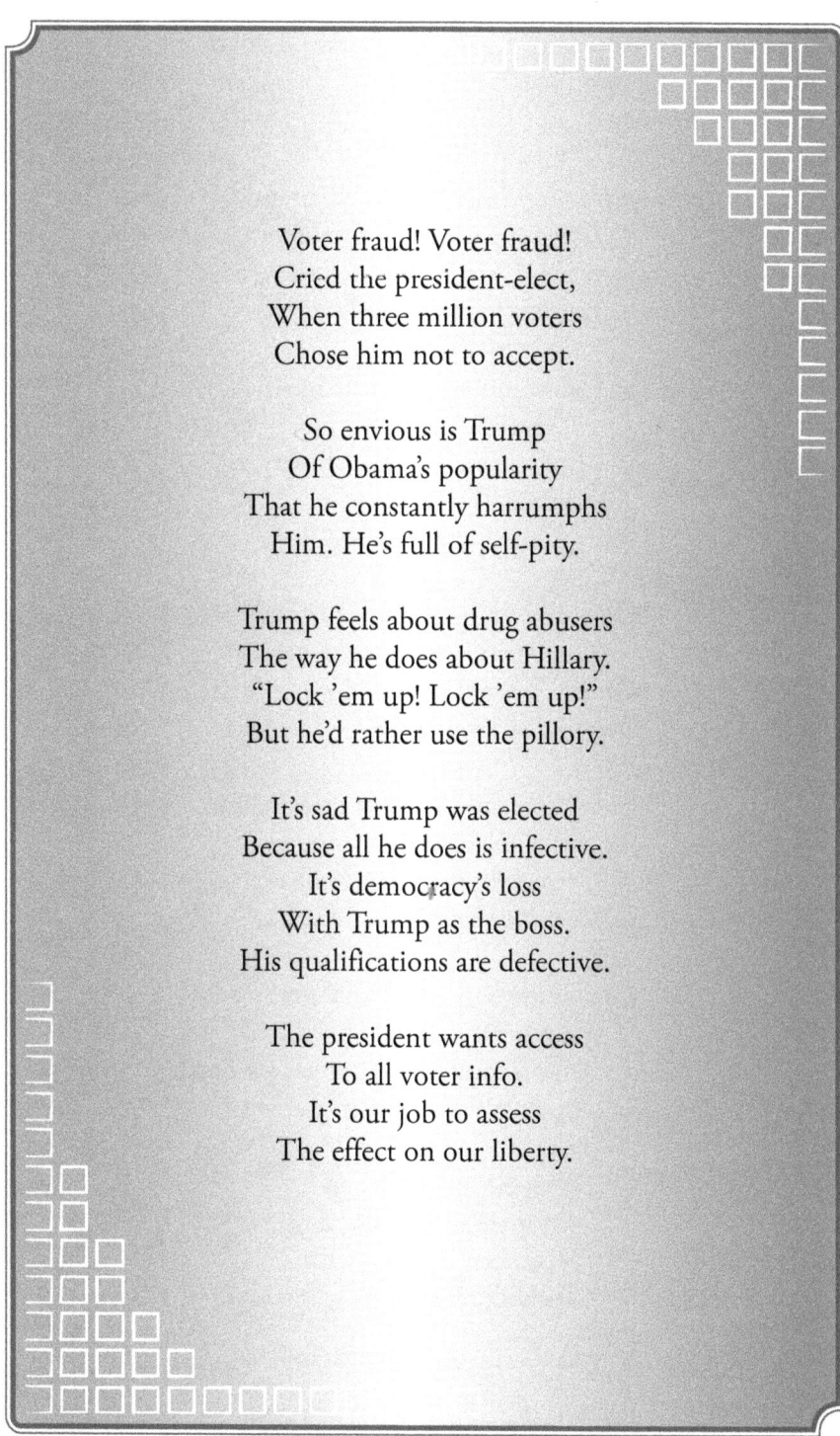

Voter fraud! Voter fraud!
Cried the president-elect,
When three million voters
Chose him not to accept.

So envious is Trump
Of Obama's popularity
That he constantly harrumphs
Him. He's full of self-pity.

Trump feels about drug abusers
The way he does about Hillary.
"Lock 'em up! Lock 'em up!"
But he'd rather use the pillory.

It's sad Trump was elected
Because all he does is infective.
It's democracy's loss
With Trump as the boss.
His qualifications are defective.

The president wants access
To all voter info.
It's our job to assess
The effect on our liberty.

"Not my fault (humility absent),"
Cries our little boy president.
I'm sure he feels the need to vent,
But without any real content.

"Make America Great Again,"
Trump wrote on a hat.
But the path he has chosen
Caused "good rule" erosion.
He's making the country go splat!

"Most important about Charlottesville
Is my very, very large winery.
Oh yes. There was a minor incident
One woman was killed by accident."

Help make my America great again.
Buy my hat for forty dollars.
I make my world great again
Whenever I make more dollars.

Lifting the ban on a lethal pesticide
To help his friend who produces it
Shows Trump cares less about planet Earth
Than he does for a person's net worth.

The pelican's beak can hold
More than his belly can.
But our bellies are full
With all of Trump's scams.

For not being killed themselves
Some give thanks to God.
But what about the seventeen
God spared not? Isn't that odd?

Belittling as a weapon
Isn't all that great.
More frequently than not
It just stirs up hate.

"Oh, what a tangled web we weave
When we first practice to deceive."
Investigations broaden,
Trump's team gets maudlin.
I'm almost certain
Time will reveal
Trump's many attempts
Our government to steal.

All of his actions
Point in that direction.
For a president, that's
A terrible infraction.

Trump is a cyst
On the butt of society.
(Maybe not nice
But I couldn't resist.)

TRUTH AND ETHICS

When truth's on vacation
There are serious implications.
Our job is much worse.
That's part of the curse
Of its absence's ramifications.

Alternative facts,
That's Trump's game.
But he pretends the press
Is doing the same.

"Fake news" is real
And here's the deal.
'Twas started by Trump and his minions.
I'm not sure there's a cure
To keep our news pure
As the right keeps spouting opinions.

Poor little narcissistic rich boy,
Troubles and woes, you've got 'em.
Poor little narcissistic rich boy,
Your ethics and morals, you forgot 'em.

The BULLY pulpit
Is well named.
The prez uses it to
Make sure others are blamed.

"The hurrier I go,
The behinder I get."
Keeping up with Trump's faux pas
Is the hardest job yet.

I want leaders
Who tell the truth.
We need good examples
For our youth.

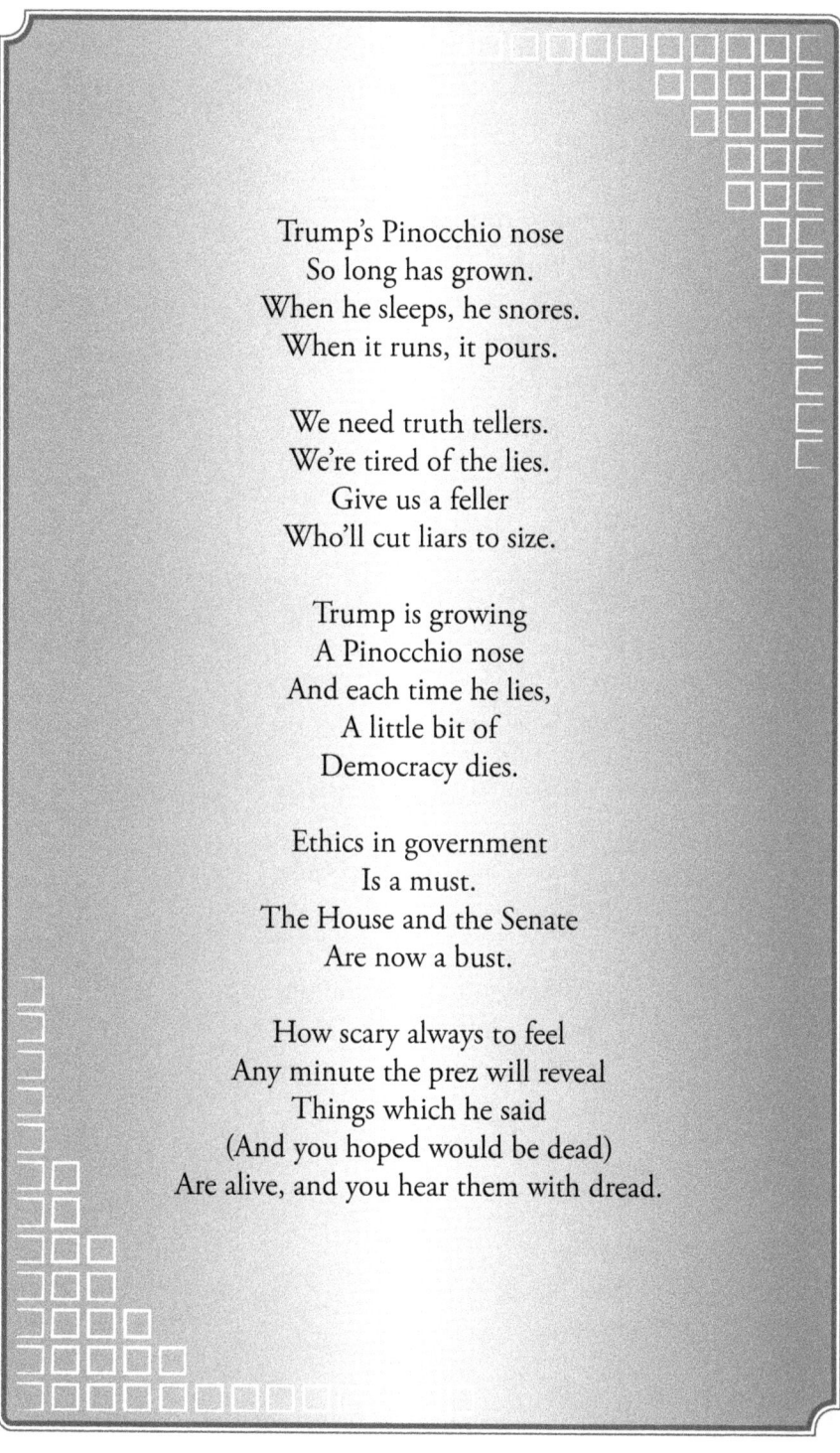

Trump's Pinocchio nose
So long has grown.
When he sleeps, he snores.
When it runs, it pours.

We need truth tellers.
We're tired of the lies.
Give us a feller
Who'll cut liars to size.

Trump is growing
A Pinocchio nose
And each time he lies,
A little bit of
Democracy dies.

Ethics in government
Is a must.
The House and the Senate
Are now a bust.

How scary always to feel
Any minute the prez will reveal
Things which he said
(And you hoped would be dead)
Are alive, and you hear them with dread.

If I were God,
One thing I would change.
All liars' noses would
Have growing pains.

We need leaders
Whose noses don't grow
Whenever they speak.
Their honesty must show.

Listening to Fox
Requires detox
To check each "fact"
For what to redact.

I tried listening to Fox
But they seldom deal in facts.
I prefer watching MSNBC
Where the truth is easier to see.

We laugh to keep our sanity
If we have to listen to Hannity.
But the underlying coup
Caused by the birther milieu
Is something we need to subdue.

If you believe
In a nation of laws,
You will consider
Corrupters outlaws.

Whenever the prez opens his mouth,
Out pops untrue statements.
He can't control his motor mouth
So he goes for personal beratements.

The more virulent the lie,
The more it gets repeated,
And if the lie is big enough
It will even be retweeted.

Giving security clearance
To those who won't divest,
Our country's secrets doth expose.
Trump can be trusted
To leak all he knows.

The emoluments clause
Is there for a reason.
Putting self before county—
Could that be called treason?

"Drain the swamp,"
Cried candidate Trump.
"I'll put them in my cabinet.
Obama's good stuff they can dump."

When Arizonians got a bellyful
Of Joe Arpaio's illegal actions,
They voted him out of office
And actually convicted him.
But Trump? He praised
And pardoned him.

Arizona sheriff Joe Arpaio
Got off scot-free.
Trump says, "Law breaking's okay
As long as you're loyal to me."

Putrid, putrefied, putrefication
Which word do you think
Best applies to T's justification
For pardoning Arpaio?
Or maybe it just plain stinks.

The 2017 federal administration
Is the most corrupt in history.
Our Trumptator thinks anything goes
As long as it's for his own glory.

According to Trump,
If your guilt you deny
We should all buy it.
So
If a woman kicks
Trump in the balls,
All she need do is deny it.

If you think allegiance
To a corrupt administration
Makes this country safer,
You are sadly mistaken.

Our elected officials
Should not be self-serving.
Tax breaks, lies, dissemination,
Though, is what we're observing.

Election integrity
Is misnamed.
It's voter suppression.
Illegals are blamed.

Twiddledee and Twiddledum.
Let's all share a bottle of rum.
Since Trump was elected,
Much truth has defected.

Trump's given to verbosity
On a little thing called Twitter.
He cares not for accuracy.
The truth away he doth fritter.

Conway and Trump
Two peas in a pod.
Both make up stuff
For the sake of effect,
But if others try it,
They want 'em to defect.

Trump shouts at the press,
"Get 'em outta here, outta here!"
And about Flynn, "Keep him in."
His priorities, we all fear,
Show no love for democracy.
Obstruction's illegal and may be a sin.

While Trump keeps us busy
(Checking his lies makes us dizzy),
The Congress passes bills
They know we won't like.
In fact, we're all in a tizzy.

The president seems determined
The investigation to quash.
What's being hidden
That he wants to kibosh?

Trump wants a pardon
But why should he care?
If he really is innocent,
He need not despair.

"Pardon me! Pardon me,"
Chants Mr. Trump.
"Oh wait. There's no need.
I can do it myself."

There's no self-pardon
So Trump should be guardin'
Against more acts criminal.
So far they're not minimal.

Investigations are intended to find
Who's guilty of things unlawful.
If the subject can pardon himself,
That's incredibly, incredibly awful.

A basketful of sycophants
(A pocketful of rye)
All willing to corrupt themselves
By promoting Donald's lies.

Admissions of ignorance
Are not an excuse
Because Comey gave Trump
Lessons profuse.

The prez refuses to learn.
Most knowledge he doth spurn.
He just keeps on twittering
And early morning frittering.

What we need is
A clean sweep.
Let's rid ourselves
Of every creep.

Condoning corruption
Seems OK with the right,
Or maybe it's power's seduction
That has put us in this plight.

Bad news proliferates.
Trump's team vituperates.
The news media reiterates.
And the country deteriorates.
But the story perpetuates
And even consolidates
That which adulterates.
Anyone for barbiturates?

President Trump
Has got to go.
Every day
His nose doth grow.

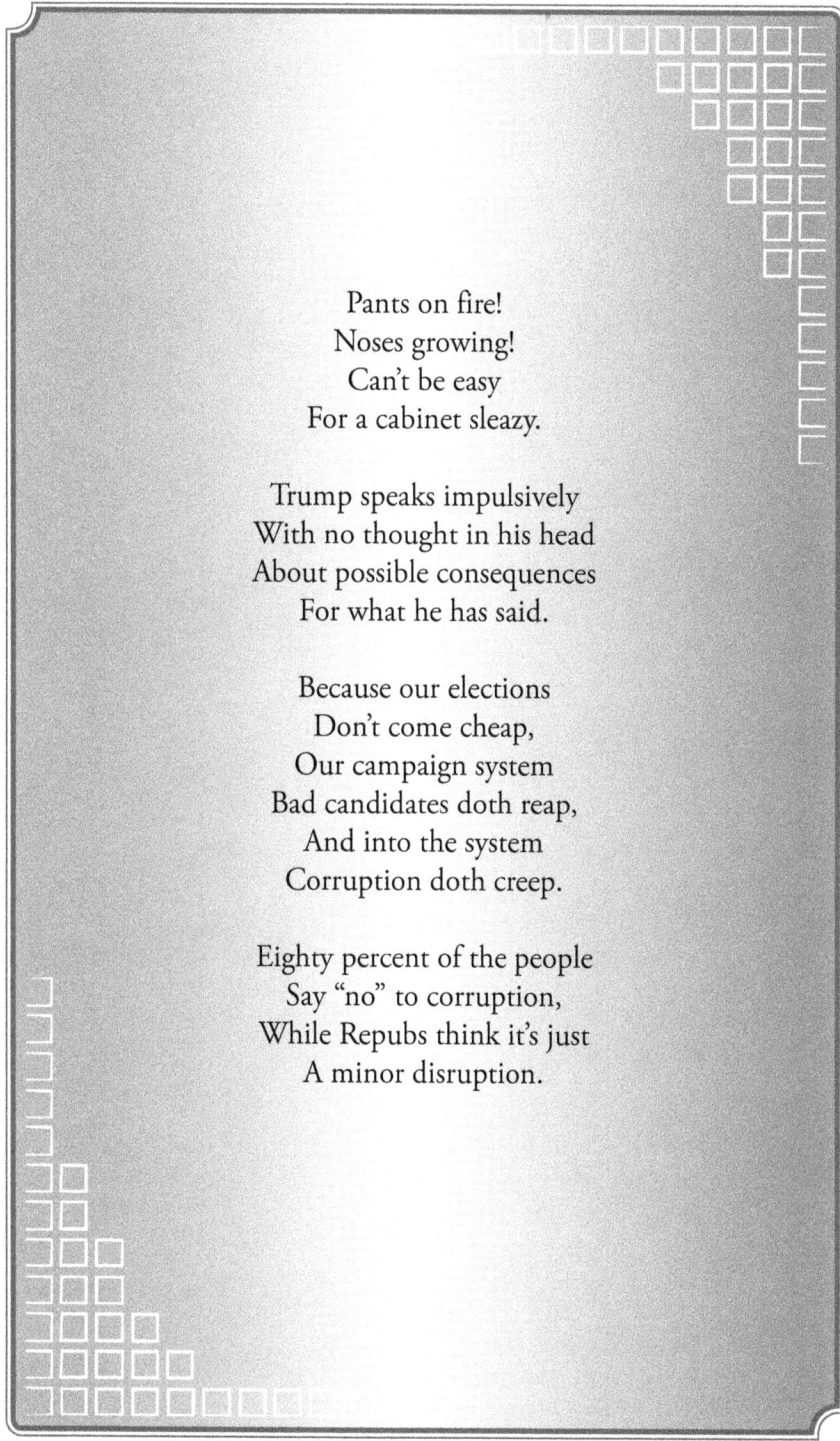

Pants on fire!
Noses growing!
Can't be easy
For a cabinet sleazy.

Trump speaks impulsively
With no thought in his head
About possible consequences
For what he has said.

Because our elections
Don't come cheap,
Our campaign system
Bad candidates doth reap,
And into the system
Corruption doth creep.

Eighty percent of the people
Say "no" to corruption,
While Repubs think it's just
A minor disruption.

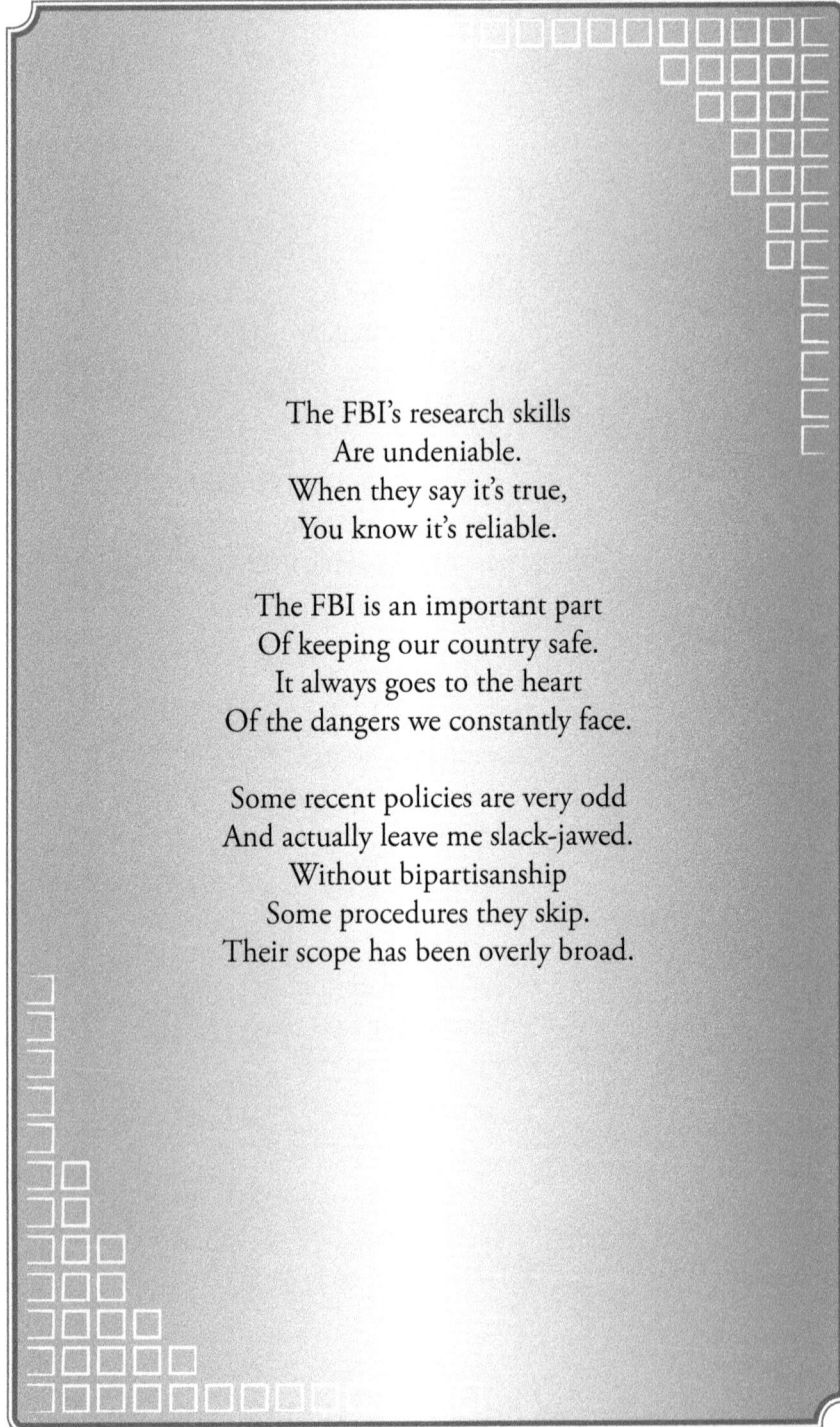

The FBI's research skills
Are undeniable.
When they say it's true,
You know it's reliable.

The FBI is an important part
Of keeping our country safe.
It always goes to the heart
Of the dangers we constantly face.

Some recent policies are very odd
And actually leave me slack-jawed.
Without bipartisanship
Some procedures they skip.
Their scope has been overly broad.

WOMEN'S ISSUES

We know from things archival
That societies all matriarchal
Of violence have less
(As I must confess)
Than societies all patriarchal.

Working diligently every week
Groups of women resisted.
Following Warren's lead
The Per-Sisters persisted.

Most maternal deaths
Should not be Texas's goal.
Closing women's clinics
Takes a deadly toll.

Alpha males
Need not fear
Alpha females
Just hold them dear!

The good ol' boys
Think they've won.
But look out, boys!
Here we come.
And hang on, boys.
We're not done.

Women have finally
Found their voices.
They're marching in droves
To expand their choices.

Discussions re women
Should not be made
Only by men
Old, white, and staid.

Free will implies free choice.
Will is only free if there *is* a choice.
Laws against choice
Give women no voice.

If men had the babies,
Perhaps they'd understand
The need for women's health care
And not just reprimands.

On denouncing abortion
The Bible says naught.
But on caring for the poor
It definitely says a lot.

Some of the Texas abortion bills
Are not only intrusive.
They are such swill,
They're actually abusive.

A Texas bill forcing women
To carry a dead fetus to term
Shows utter disdain for
The health and psyche of women.
But old men keep singing this refrain.

The old male Bible-thumpers
Should *read* the book they follow,
Because many of their arguments
Are incorrect and hollow.

There is nothing in the Bible
About fetal abortion,
But anal religionists
Blow it out of proportion.

Burdening Texas women
(Who naturally miscarry)
With rules on remains interment
Is scary! Be very, very wary!

Laws re carrying
A dead fetus to term
Show utter ignorance.
But GOP (Texas) holds firm
While the rest of us squirm.

What's good for the goose
Should be good for the gander.
But Trump's attitudes induce
Most women to say "Vamoose!"

"Little Miss Muffet
Sat on a tuffet
Eating her curds and whey."
Y'all take note,
She should go vote!
Better to have say than whey.

Imagine Trump
Stalking Oprah on the debate stage.
Slowly she turns, without any rage,
Hands on her hip
Smiling sweetly, she says,
"Donald honey.
Go stand by your mike
And wait your turn.
This space is mine.
Your hovering I spurn."

Trump, who loves conspiracy theories,
Keeps making them up to tweet.
Anyone with whom he's a beef
Can expect to receive endless tweets.

Tweet! Tweet! Tweet!
And constantly repeat.

Too much testosterone we deride.
More estrogen some balance would provide.
Did you ever hear two women decide,
"Let's just take it all outside"?

MISCELLANEOUS

I remember World War II
With FDR. Now there was a leader.
We all worked together,
And that pulled us through.

The birther milieu
Back in 2008
When T started his smear
Was the public beginning
Of this continuing coup.

Understanding of others
Obviously is a must
Before making laws
You expect us to trust.

Russia helped Trump get elected.
He claims his campaign wasn't affected.
But if the indictment you've inspected,
His final election was to be expected.

There once was a man named Spicer
Who agreed to be Trump's liefer.
Desperate his job to keep
The president's lies he did leak
And kept lying, much to our pique.
Or
The prez's lies he did lob.
'Twas part of his job.
He became T's main crowd sizer.

Threatened with his loss of job
Spicer agreed T's lies to lob.
When he lied about crowd size,
We saw it was false by our own eyes.

Just when it seemed
Things were somewhat improving,
Along came a prez
Who's beyond the pale.
He's completely disapproving
Of anyone not white and male.

CONCLUSIONS

Shooting our political opponents
Is definitely not the solution.
Listening, debating all components,
And compromise is my solution.

Dinosaurs? We have a few.
The filibuster, redistricting,
The electoral college too.
Why not dump them all
And restructure them anew?

There's a war in the States
That comes not from abroad.
It'll take work and resistance.
All efforts we applaud.

Hundreds of lives have been lost
And yet we must pay the cost
Of Congress' recusal
And the NRA's refusal
To regulate arms and stem the loss.

Let's have one bill, one vote
With no extraneous additions.
It would save time, we should note,
And be a far less confusing rendition.

Twiddledee and Twiddledum.
Give us each a bottle of rum.
Obstruction of justice and obfuscation
Make us want to upchuck our ration.

Government by absurdity
Only lasts so long. Heaven knows
Someone needs to tell the prez
He's not wearing any clothes.

Trump could choose to resign.
If he chooses to stay,
It must be our way:
No tyrannical actions,
No warring factions,
No more brazen lies,
And no protecting Russian spies.

So philosophically divided are we
That a two-state division
May be the only revision
Some US voters can see.

My advice to those who hate
Our democratic way of life:
Pick a country and repatriate
Because the haters here cause strife.

Working diligently every week,
A group of women resisted.
Following Elizabeth Warren's lead,
The Per-Sisters persisted.

Senator Warren refused to "sit down!"
Eventually, she did comply and frowned.
"I may be sitting on the outside,
But I'm standing up on the inside."

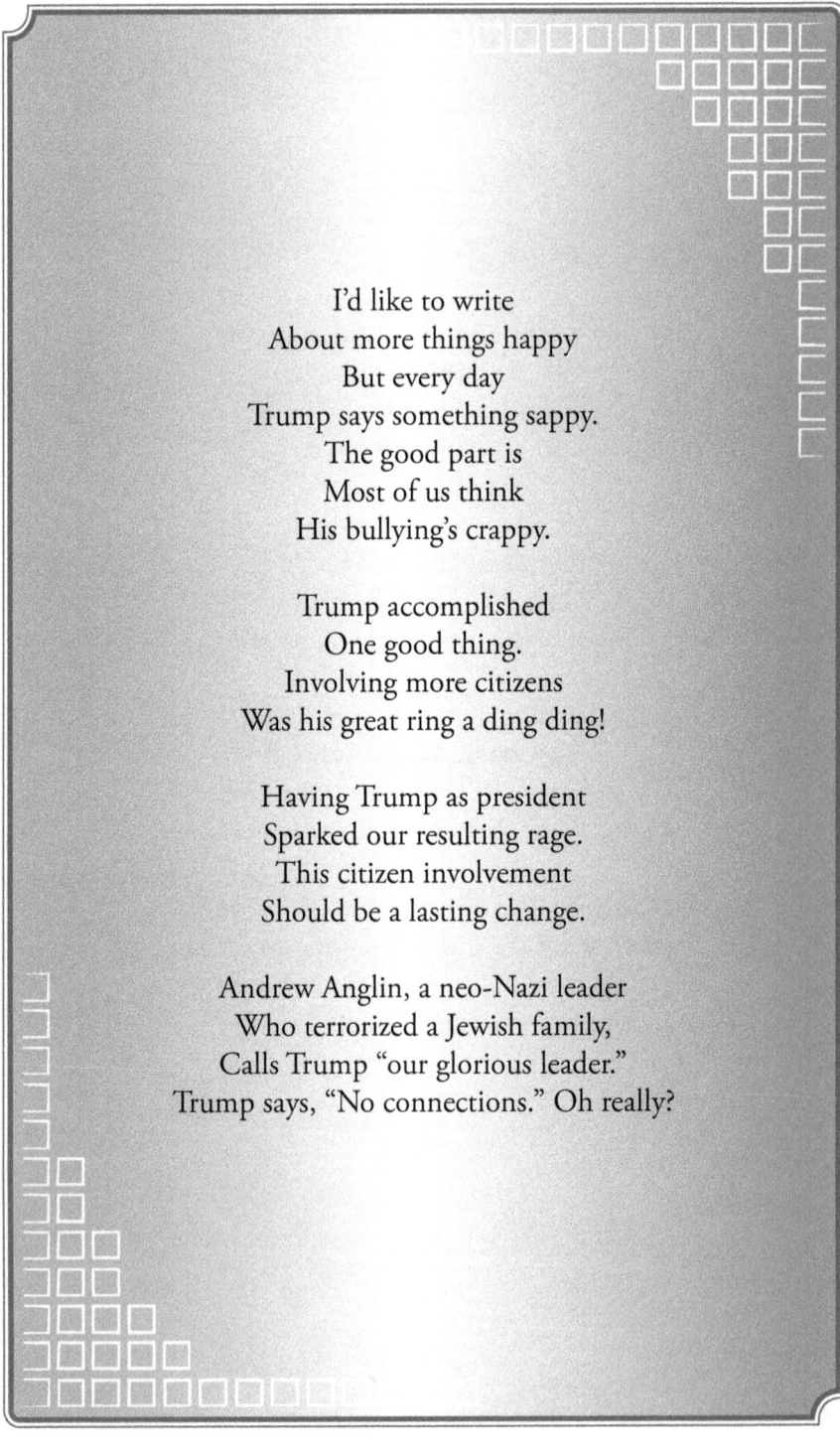

I'd like to write
About more things happy
But every day
Trump says something sappy.
The good part is
Most of us think
His bullying's crappy.

Trump accomplished
One good thing.
Involving more citizens
Was his great ring a ding ding!

Having Trump as president
Sparked our resulting rage.
This citizen involvement
Should be a lasting change.

Andrew Anglin, a neo-Nazi leader
Who terrorized a Jewish family,
Calls Trump "our glorious leader."
Trump says, "No connections." Oh really?

If you want a country
That's just plain white
Join the Nazis and alt-right
And let the rest of us be free.

We fought a world war
Against the Nazi whore.
Why now let her loose again
And allow those ideas to soar?

Rolling his eyes
At things Trump said,
Japan's prime minister
Tried carefully to tread.

Nunes refused recusal.
He's staying in the loop.
He keeps releasing fake news,
Hoping some of you he can dupe.

Our infrastructure is a mess.
Much of it needs to be replaced.
But for that, I must confess,
Most of the Congress has no taste.

Our levees are old
And need redoing.
Unless we work together,
More problems will be ensuing.

I don't trust anyone
Who doesn't like animals.
The current White House
Has animus, but not animals.

McCain, a Republican,
Is an honorable man.
Even so he admits-----whoa,
He sometimes puts party-----oh,
Over the country he loves so.

The Democratic platform
Is a spiritual document for me.
The Republican platform?
A desecration of values, I see.

There's no question in my mind
That Trump is acting for Russia.
Everything he has done shows
He's trying to hand us to Russia.

In their ignorance
Trump's voters have agreed
They want Russia
To take over our country.

Trump's voters colluded,
Though their wits were denuded,
To invalidate democracy
In favor of autocracy.

I voted for Hillary,
And I'd do it again.
She had the right stance
But Repubs, in a trance,
Did the Donald J. dance.
And now bad policies advance.

Trump is a traitor.
No other way to say it,
For actions he has taken,
To take our country and fillet it.

For eight full years
Republicans refused
To work with Democrats.
They wrote no bills
To cure our ills.
They added no bills to the stats.

With missiles a flyin'
We need rational voices.
Don't want to be cryin'
Because of bad choices.

"In order to keep my sanity,
Nineteen holes is what I prefer."
Don't worry, Mr. President.
You're still as sane as you ever were.

Out with the old.
In with the new.
Of great candidates
We have quite a few.

If Obama did it,
Repubs will kill it.
They'll reword the idea
And then rebill it.

Anti-Semitic acts rose dramatically
After Donald Trump was elected.
Perpetrators showed emphatically
It was Trump's attitudes they'd selected.

Elections are hard enough to monitor
Without help from the Russians.
That they hacked us is evident
And requires more discussions.

Sabotage is a word
We use with an enemy.
The right uses it the FBI to destroy.
Camouflage is a word we use to cover up.
Sabotage, camouflage is
A 2018 alt-right ploy.

If you don't vote,
There's not much hope
For us to cope
With this slippery slope.

If you don't vote,
Don't complain.
You'll have a government by rote
That you'll have to explain.

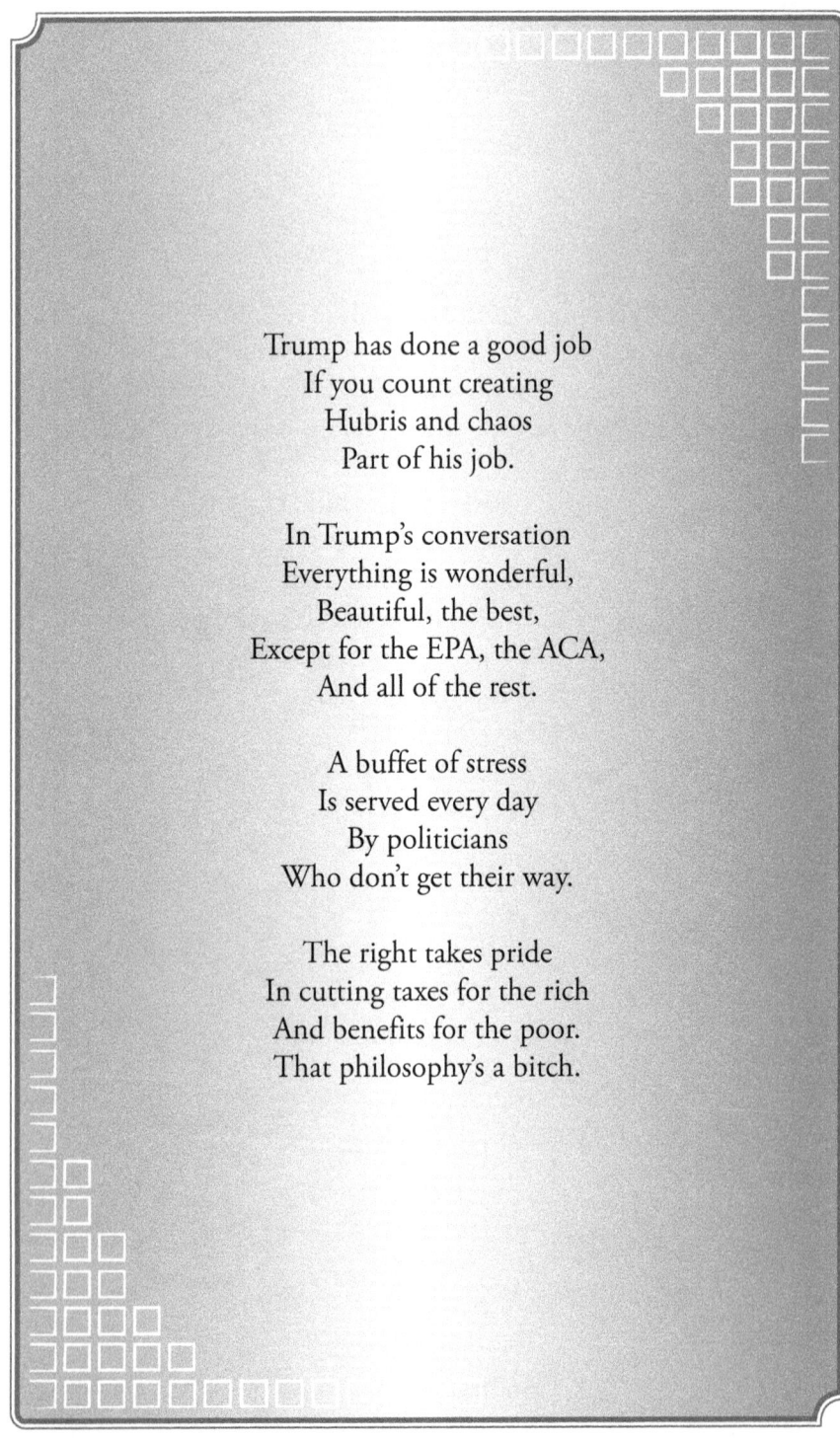

Trump has done a good job
If you count creating
Hubris and chaos
Part of his job.

In Trump's conversation
Everything is wonderful,
Beautiful, the best,
Except for the EPA, the ACA,
And all of the rest.

A buffet of stress
Is served every day
By politicians
Who don't get their way.

The right takes pride
In cutting taxes for the rich
And benefits for the poor.
That philosophy's a bitch.

To run for public office
There should be prerequisites:
Civics test and psych tests and
Common sense would be exquisite.

"I promise coal jobs"
Even if they kill us
(Or turn our lungs to big black globs).
T's such an ignorant cuss.

Ignorance as an excuse for Trump
Simply won't cut it.
On the campaign trail, he bragged
About being so smart.
And millions of you dug it.

We've peaked in our evolution
If you think Trump's the solution
To problems long standing
(Much thought they're demanding).
Going backward seems Donald's conclusion.

I've vented a lot
Writing my thoughts.
Now it's time to heal
And some unity reveal.

Our democracy is worth the effort,
But way more energy we must exert.
So let's overcome our fear
And democracy revere.

About the Author

Val Richardson became interested in politics late in life after moving to Rowlett, Texas. In 2016, she worked tangentially for Hillary Clinton, determined to live long enough to see the first woman president sworn in. When Trump unexpectedly won the election, Val took serious notice and decided that she needed to hang around at least two more years in order to work in the resistance and help the Democrats dominate the midterms and salvage our democracy.

Thus began her efforts to help the best candidates in Texas. She wrote some rhymes favoring progressives and used them in tweets, e-mails, and postcards and then just kept on writing. At the same time, she hosted a weekly political action group consisting of a few dedicated women who called themselves the Per-Sisters in honor of Elizabeth Warren and other strong women who continue to fight for women's rights and other important issues.

CPSIA information can be obtained
at www.ICGtesting.com
Printed in the USA
FFHW01n0023190918
48489958-52347FF

9 781643 504131